GLASS ETCHING
SURFACE TECHNIQUES AND DESIGNS

Page 49

NORMAN DOBBINS & DEBRA FELBERG OXLEY

CKE Publications
Olympia, Washington

Page 63 *Positive etch on window glass.*

Page 66 *Reverse etch on blue/clear flashed glass.*

Page 71 *Positive etch on window glass.*

Page 46 *Reverse etch on red/clear flashed glass.*

Page 73 *Positive etch on window glass.*

Page 45 *Reverse etch on red/clear flashed glass.*

Page 43 *Reverse etch on red/clear flashed glass. A decorative crescent shape was left unblasted for additional design interest.*

Page 72 *Positive etch on window glass.*

Page 89

Left:
Double doors have a positive etch on 1/4" safety laminated glass inserts.

Below:
The background design from page 74 has been reversed in the right window for a different look. Birds from pages 75 and 77, one of them reversed, were inserted into the background scene.

Pages 74, 75, and 77

Page 82 *Door insert with positive etch on 1/4" safety laminated glass.*
CKE-123 DRAGON *full-size pattern, see page 96.*

Page 83 *Door insert with positive etch on 1/4" safety laminated glass. Foliage has been extended into the transom overhead.*
CKE-124 CHERRY BLOSSOMS *full-size pattern, see page 96.*

Page 60 *Reverse etch on white/clear flashed glass.*

Page 90 *Reverse etch on pink/clear flashed glass.*

Page 56 *Wood box with etched top.*

Page 42 *Positive etch on window glass with oak frame.*

Page 59 *Oak bookends with etched 1/4" plate glass inserts.*
Page 68 *Oak pen holder with 1/4" plate glass insert. Design is reversed with the wave configuration modified for the half-circle shape.*

Page 85 *Oak end table with etched 1/4" plate glass top.*

Page 39 *Crab* **Page 32** *Tulips* **Page 39** *Iris* **Page 39** *Crocus*
All are positive etch on square or rectangular beveled glass.

Page 51 *Iris* **Page 59** *Wild Rose* **Page 50** *Lilies*
All are positive etch on oval beveled glass.

Many of the smaller designs are interchangeable on beveled glass diamonds, squares, circles, ovals, and other shapes. When framed with brass or zinc came and hung in a window they make exceptionally beautiful suncatchers.

Page 41 *Tulips*   **Page 65** *Top Lily*   **Page 64** *Iris*   **Page 40** *Bottom Lily*
All are positive etch on circular beveled glass.

Page 58   *Positive etch on octagon beveled glass.*

Page 92 and 93

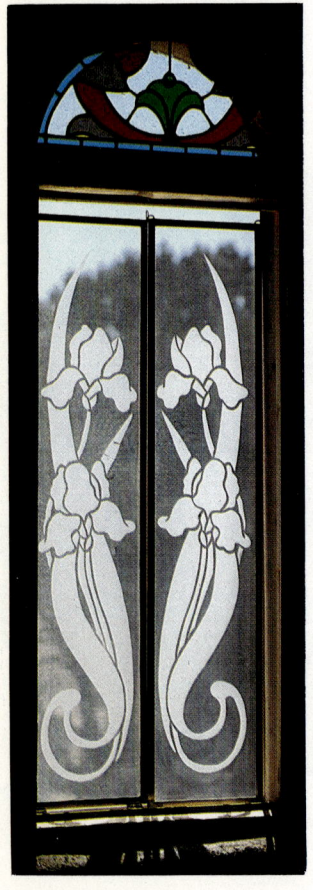

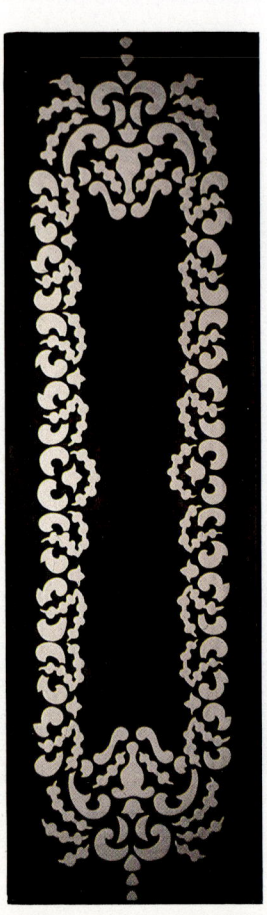

Above:
Oriental panels as a three-section screen or room divider. Reverse etched inserts on 1/4" plate glass. Each panel is suitable to be used separately as a sidelight or other type of windows. Available as full-size patterns, see page 96:

CKE-125 BAMBOO A, *(left panel)*
CKE-126 BAMBOO B, *(center panel)*
CKE-127 BAMBOO C, *(right panel)*

Far Left:
Positive etch on window glass with the design reversed in the second panel.

Left:
Positive etch on 1/4" plate glass.

Page 86   Page 88

GLASS ETCHING
SURFACE TECHNIQUES AND DESIGNS

NORMAN DOBBINS & DEBRA FELBERG OXLEY

CKE Publications
Olympia, Washington

Acknowledgements

Many of the projects in this book were made possible through the generosity of the companies listed below. Their products are available at many stained glass shops and we encourage you to ask for them by name.

We also wish to extend special thanks to Butch Young. Without her help in producing many of the projects in this book, it would have taken much longer to get the job done.

Norman Dobbins and Debra Oxley

Credits
Wood tables and screens: Northern Hardwood Frames
Wood frames: McNeil Custom Woods
Pen stand, bookends, wood boxes: Clarity Glass Design
Glass, resist materials: National Sandblast Systems, Ltd.

Cover Design, Production Graphics: Jessie Colter
Publication Design: Carolyn Kyle
Photography: Norman Dobbins
Color: Colour Scan, Inc.; Portland, Oregon
Printing: Williams Catello Printing, Inc.; Tualatin, Oregon

Copyright © CKE PUBLICATIONS, 1988.
2840-E Black Lake Blvd., Olympia, WA 98502

Copyright © Norman Dobbins, 1988.
Covers text portion of this book.

Copyright © Debra Felberg Oxley, 1988.
Covers all designs in this book.

ISBN 0-935133-23-2

ALL RIGHTS RESERVED. No part of this publication may be reproduced, stored or transmitted in any form or by any means, electronic, mechanical, recording or otherwise, without the prior permission of the copyright owners, with the exception of reproduction of the patterns for personal use only.

Distribution:
CKE PUBLICATIONS
2840-E Black Lake Blvd.
Olympia, WA 98502
(206) 352-4427

Table of Contents

Section I TECHNIQUES FOR SURFACE ETCHING

Chapter 1 UNDERSTANDING GLASS ETCHING — 5
Why Glass Etching? What is Glass Etching?

Chapter 2 THE DESIGN AND THE GLASS — 7
Preparing the Design: Converting a Line Drawing to a Block Design, Enlarging the Design, Using an Enlarging Copier, Using an Opaque Projector, Using an Overhead Projector, Using a Blueprint Shop; **Selecting the Glass:** Safety Glass, Clear, Colorless Glass, Colored Glass; **Cleaning the Glass**

Chapter 3 PREPARATION FOR ETCHING — 10
Choosing a Resist: Toughness, Ease of Transfer, Type of Adhesive, Alternate Resists; **Applying the Resist; Transfering the Design:** Carbon or Graphite Paper, Graphite Transfer, Spray Adhesive; **Cutting the Design**

Chapter 4 THE SANDBLASTING PROCESS — 14
Preparing to Sandblast, The Blasting Process, Checking for Quality, Finishing Up

Chapter 5 NOW WHAT CAN YOU MAKE? — 16
Home Decorating, Gifts, Stained Glass Windows, Wood Accessories, Signs, Commercial Uses, Art Glass

Section II GLASS ETCHING EQUIPMENT & SAFETY PROCEDURES

Chapter 6 COMPRESSORS — 17
Electrical Requirements for Compressors: Single Phase vs. Three Phase, Pressure Per Square Inch, Horsepower, Single and Two-stage Compressors; **The Air Tank; Gasoline Compressors**

Chapter 7 SANDBLASTERS AND ABRASIVES — 20
Sandblasters: The Siphon System, The Pressure System; **Determining Air Requirements; Abrasives:** Sand, Garnet, Aluminum Oxide, Silicon Carbide, Glass Beads

Chapter 8 BLASTING CABINENTS — 24

Chapter 9 SAFETY EQUIPMENT — 25
Protection for Your Head and Neck, Protection for Your Lungs, Protection for your Ears

Chapter 10 IN CONCLUSION — 26

Section III DESIGNS FOR ETCHING — 27

Full-size Pattern Ordering Information — 96

INTRODUCTION

This book is unique because it is the first one to present a complete approach to learning one glass etching technique with an abundance of designs included. Its purpose is threefold: first to show how easy and rewarding it is to learn surface glass etching; second to completely explain the equipment and safety procedures necessary; and third to provide you with high quality etching designs to try on your own.

Writing the book has been an interesting challenge. Norm has taught intensive glass etching seminars for several years with each one presenting in-depth information on technique, design, equipment, and safety. The seminar format allowed lots of time for detailed information and question answering. In the book format, however, "wordy" explanations had to be done away with and all of the information concisely presented in the space allotted. The book had to be clear enough for beginning glass etchers but be in-depth to the extent that it would also be helpful to experienced etchers. In other words, we tried to give all the basics and then more.

In addition to a broad base of information, we wanted the designs to run the gamut from very basic to advanced. Debbie worked very hard to get the right balance as she designed a range of simple to complex designs with a wide variety of subject matter. We hope you decide that the designs alone are reason enough to have this book in your library, even if you are already experienced in glass etching.

We have provided color photographs of as many of the finished designs as we could, so you can actually see how they are supposed to look. In doing this, we tried to use as many different types of glass in as many different types of projects as possible. Only in this way did we feel that we could convey an idea of the full range of possibilities available for etched glass.

We hope that we have succeeded in presenting a book that will be useful to you not only now but for many years. In addition, we hope that you will be so excited about etching that you will want to go on to the more advanced etching techniques also.

SECTION I
TECHNIQUES FOR SURFACE ETCHING

This section will give all the basic techniques necessary for surface etching. By reading and following them closely you will, right from the beginning, build into your work correct habits which will lead to consistently professional results.

Step one will be to carefully choose and then to prepare the design. Once this is done, the choice and preparation of glass deserves good attention. The final step of actually sandblasting will take less time than the first two but its success is very dependent on how well the first two were accomplished. A careful sandblasting job will round out your efforts and lead you to a beautifully etched finished project.

Chapter 1
UNDERSTANDING GLASS ETCHING

Why glass etching?

Etching is a beautiful way to decorate the surface of a piece of glass. It is elegant and expressive in a way that is far out of proportion to the ease of producing it. In other words, it is much easier to do than you would suspect by looking at the finished product. The basic form of etching is called surface etching and it is where we will start our series of books on the art of glass etching. The more sophisticated techniques of carving and shading will be covered completely in the second and third books.

There has been an incredible surge of interest in etched glass in recent years, both from consumers and from artists. Consumers have discovered that etched glass is a beautiful and elegant art form of its own as well as an affordable alternative to stained glass. Glass artists have discovered that there is a ready market for etched glass but they have also discovered that etching provides them with a medium which is not limited by the restrictions of stained glass. They can now design without having to worry about extraneous lead lines - indeed, without lead lines at all. They never have to worry if a piece of glass can be cut to a certain shape because designs can be etched to any shape. They also don't have to worry about parts of a design being too small to cut and lead (or foil) since etched designs can have elements almost as small as you can discern with the naked eye.

Another bonus is that etching is so much faster to do than stained glass. This means that, both for the hobbiest and the artist, the gratification of seeing the completed piece comes much faster. It also means that a finished piece can be sold for less than a stained glass piece of comparable complexity while generating more money per hour for the artist doing it. This provides one of those all too rare win/win situations where the consumer is happy because he pays less for a good product and the artist is happy because he makes more money doing it.

Surface etching is the easiest and most basic type of glass etching to learn - but that doesn't mean you can't make some really beautiful projects using the technique. The complexity and artistic merit of the design are as important as the type of technique used to produce the finished etching. Many glass etchers only surface etch for the first two or three years they are etching glass before they try any of the more sophisticated techniques. This is due in part to the lack of instruction available in the other techniques and in part to the lack of knowledge about the proper type of equipment to use. However, in large measure it is due to the inherent satisfaction people get with surface etching and the vast number of different types of projects which can be done with surface etching. It just takes a long time to explore the full potential of one technique.

In this book we will show you surface etching from A to Z. We will cover the techniques, the products and the equipment you need along with the safety precautions you should take. We have also provided you with over eighty different designs to try yourself. Even if you are already an experienced glass etcher, this book has something for you.

What Is Glass Etching?

Glass etching is the abrading or roughening of the surface of a piece of glass in selected areas in order to produce a desired design. There are two general types of glass etching - sandblast etching and acid etching*. For the purposes of this book, we will use the term "etching" to refer specifically to sandblast etching. Sandblast etching provides more different types of effects, is easier to learn, and is generally less dangerous to do than is acid etching.

The etched effect is produced by directing a high pressure, high speed stream of sand (or other abrasive) at the surface of a piece of glass. When the grains of abrasive hit the surface of the glass with enough force, they chip tiny bits of glass out of the surface, leaving a white, frosted look. The design is produced by protecting the surface of the glass in the areas you do not wish to be etched with a resist material, while leaving the areas of the surface exposed which you do wish to be etched. When the sandblasting is completed, the protected areas remain clear and the areas which were not protected are etched.

Just about any type of glass can be etched - clear window glass, plate glass in any thickness, laminated glass, mirror, stained glass, flashed glass, and glassware of all types. The only type of glass you need to be wary of is *tempered glass*. This is basically clear glass which has been heat treated to create tremendous tension in the glass. The reason for this is that when a piece of tempered glass is broken, it breaks into thousands of tiny bits instead of a few large pieces. Tempered glass is considered safety glass because it is stronger than non tempered glass of the same thickness and if it is broken, those thousands of tiny pieces will do much less harm to anyone they happen to hit than they would if they were much larger and heavier. If tempered glass is etched more than very lightly on the surface, the inner tensions may be released and the glass might shatter on the spot. Sometimes a piece of tempered glass is etched and doesn't shatter until days or weeks later. So, it is wise to stay away from tempered glass unless you have been etching long enough to be able to have very fine control of your sandblaster. *(If you are not sure how to tell if a piece of glass is tempered, look in all the corners of the piece of glass. If it is tempered it should have a notice stenciled onto the glass to that effect in one corner, in an area about 1/2" x 1".)*

Almost any type of object made out of glass in any shape can be etched, and the list of possibilities is practically endless. For example: glass in windows and doors, kitchen cabinets, bathroom medicine chests, glass shelves, mirrors, glass firescreens, room dividers, table tops, boxes, paperweights, pencil and pen sets, nameplates, wine glasses, beer mugs, decanters, bottles, coasters, Christmas ornaments, suncatchers, fused glass objects, bowls, and plates to name a few. It is particularly nice to be able to personalize glass gift items by etching the name or monogram of the recipient on it, or a date or saying which is significant to that person.

We have included patterns in this book which are suitable for etching on many of these items and we have provided photographs of as many finished pieces as possible.

---

*Acid etching is accomplished by the use of hydrofluoric acid, which is a very dangerous chemical and one to be avoided unless you are well trained in its use. A type of very light etching can also be produced with the different types of etching creams that are commonly available in many stained glass and hobby supply stores. These etching creams contain a modified and "toned down" form of hydrofluoric acid which is safer to use if the directions are carefully followed. The effect produced by these creams is not as high quality as that produced by sandblast etching and it is difficult to avoid an irregular or splotched look in the larger areas of a design when using them.

Chapter 2
THE DESIGN AND THE GLASS

Preparing the Design

In surface etching, there are only two visual elements that make up all finished pieces - the etched areas and the clear areas. This appears to the eye as frosted and clear, with the etched areas appearing frosted and the non-etched areas appearing clear. With surface etching, you can etch your designs in two different ways. First, you can do a positive etch, which means that the main subject of the design is etched and the background is clear. A reverse etch means that the subject is left clear and the background is etched.

What this means in either case is that all of the areas of your design which are to be etched and which should be distinct from each other must be separated from each other by a clear space. Any parts that touch, with no clear space between, will blend together with no indication of where one stops and the other starts.

When you are preparing the design for a surface etched piece, you can most easily visualize what it will look like if you work from a black and white block design rather than a line drawing. If you work from a line drawing, particularly if it is a moderately complicated one, it will be very difficult to tell which parts of the design will be etched and which will be left clear. Once you gain experience, you will be more comfortable working with line drawings, but in the beginning you will have a far easier time with block designs. *(All the designs included in this book are block designs.)*

Converting a Line Drawing to a Block Design

If the design you want to etch is in the form of a line drawing, with all the elements touching, it will be necessary to convert the design to block form with the elements separated. The easiest way to do this is to put the original on a light table with tracing paper over it. You then go over each element of the design, shading them in but leaving a space between each one. Another way to do this if you don't have a light table, is to use carbon paper and trace the original design onto another piece of paper, leaving a space between each element. If you do it this way, you will still have a line drawing, but there will be a double line between each element, indicating the clear space between them. It is this double line between elements which is confusing, so you would be better off to go ahead and shade in the areas to be etched.

It will be much easier to tell which areas of resist to peel off the glass if you work from a block design rather than a line drawing.

7

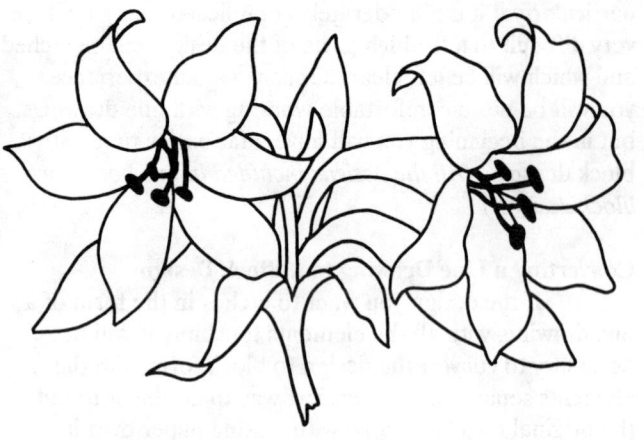 

A line drawing or other artwork must be converted to a block design before proceeding with preparation for etching.

Enlarging the Design

Once you have your design in block form, you will have to enlarge it to the size you want the finished etching. You can do this in one of several ways.

Using an Enlarging Copier

If the finished size is not over 22" x 34", you can use an enlarging copier at your local copy shop. Most of these copiers can use paper up to 11" x 17" and you can enlarge your design in sections and tape the sections together. This can get difficult if you have to enlarge your design into more than four sections to tape together, hence the 22" x 34" size limitation. *(Of course, four sections could be put together to produce a piece 11" x 68" or 17" x 44".)* Some copy shops have copiers made especially for large scale enlarging. They automatically produce segmented enlargements up to 11" x 17" which tape together well with very little overlap.

Using an Opaque Projector

A second way to enlarge your pattern is to use an opaque projector. If you don't happen to have one, you can usually rent one inexpensively from an office supply or school supply store. Some stained glass shops also sell and rent opaque projectors. You use this projector to project your black and white design on a smooth wall which you have thoughtfully covered with a large piece of white paper. You can move the projector closer to or farther from the wall to decrease or increase the size of the image. When you get the exact size image you want, simply trace the design onto the piece of paper.

Using an Overhead Projector

An overhead projector will do the same thing as an opaque projector, but your original design must be on clear film instead of white paper. If you can more easily locate an overhead projector than an opaque projector, an easy way to convert your design from black on white to black on clear film is to copy the design onto clear film at your local copyshop. Most copyshops have this film *(usually acetate)* available.

Using a Blueprint Shop

Another way to enlarge your pattern is to take it to a blueprint shop and have them enlarge it for you. They may have to go through several stages of enlargement, depending on how large your oringinal is and how much you want it enlarged. This is the most expensive process for enlargement.

All these processes for enlarging designs will distort the design slightly. In most cases, the distortion is so slight as to be unnoticeable. You will have to be particularly careful, however, if you have a geometric design. You will find that when enlarging most geometric designs, some corrections are necessary to maintain square corners and perfectly straight lines.

When working on your design it is important to remember that you can etch on both sides of a piece of glass. In many cases, you will find it desirable to etch on the back of the glass even though the etching will be viewed from the front. Any time this situation occurs, remember that the design will be reversed when you view the finished product. If you have lettering in the design, remember to reverse the lettering on the design itself, so that it will read correctly on the finished etching.

Selecting the Glass

Now that you have your design enlarged to the desired size, the next step is to select and prepare the glass. Just about any type of glass can be etched except tempered glass. The most common types of glass used for etching are double strength *(1/8" thick)* window glass, 1/4" plate glass, 1/8" or 1/4" mirror, laminated safety glass and flashed stained glass.

Safety Glass

If you are producing an etching which will be installed in a location where your building codes require safety glass, try to use laminated safety glass rather than tempered glass. Laminated glass is two layers of thinner glass, held together by a layer of clear epoxy in between to produce a single piece of thicker glass which is stronger and which will not fall apart when broken. There is no danger in surface etching laminated glass while there may be a danger of shattering tempered glass when it is etched. Experienced glass etchers seem to have good luck with tempered glass if they only very lightly etch the surface of the glass, but it is not recommended for a beginner *(see Chapter I)*.

Clear Colorless Glass

In selecting the glass you will be etching, if you want glass that is clear and has no color, you will use either double strength, 1/4" plate or laminated glass. Double strength is usually used for smaller pieces, up to about five square feet. Plate glass is used in larger pieces or where there will be stress on the glass, such as an outside window where there is a lot of wind. Laminated glass is used where it is required by the building code or where there is a higher probability of breakage, such as a window in a door or beside a door.

Colored Glass

If you want to incorporate color in your etching, there are two ways to do it. You can etch on translucent stained glass, producing two shades of the same color. This is most effective if the glass has as little texture on the surface as possible, since a textured surface distorts the etching. A most effective way to incorporate color is to use flashed glass. This is a type of handblown glass, which has a thick base layer of clear or light color glass and a thin layer or "flash" of darker color glass on top. You always etch on the flashed side of the glass, and you usually etch deeply enough to completely remove the layer of flashed color. This gives you a two color etching with one piece of glass, the color of the base glass where the flash was removed with the flash color remaining where the glass was protected by the resist.

Cleaning the Glass

Before resist can be applied to the glass in preparation for etching, the glass must be thoroughly cleaned so the resist will stick well. The cleaning of all of these different types of glass is the same except for mirror. That is, you must thoroughly clean the side of the glass that you are going to etch. You can use commercial window cleaner for this purpose on all the different types of glass except on the back of mirror. Some commercial cleaners contain chemicals which will eventually darken or discolor the mirror backing, so it is best to use alcohol on the back of mirror.

Once the surface to be etched has been cleaned, it is ready for the application of the resist material, which is the subject of the next chapter.

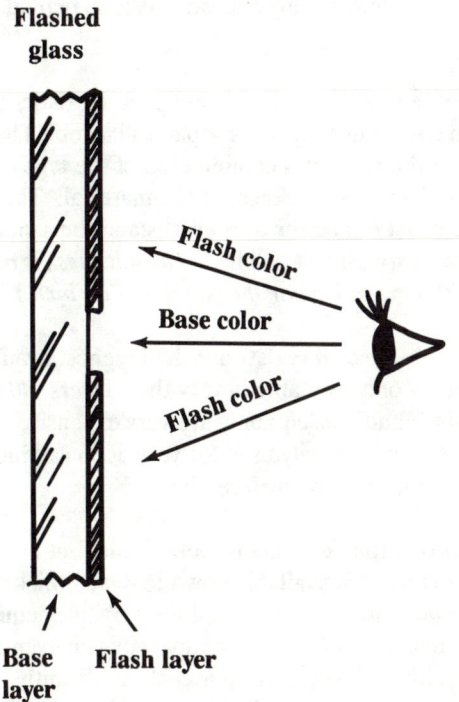

Cross section of a piece of flashed glass:
The predominant color in flashed glass comes from the thin layer of flashed color. When you etch through the flash layer, you see the color of the base layer underneath.

Chapter 3
PREPARATION FOR ETCHING

Choosing a Resist

Before the a design can be etched on the glass, a resist material has to be applied to the glass to protect the areas which are not to be etched. A resist is simply anything which resists the effects of the sand and protects the glass. In most cases the resist which is used is a type of self adhesive vinyl, polyethylene, or rubber which can be easily applied to the glass.

The best types of resist are especially designed for glass etching. They are tough and resilient, repelling the sand particles long enough for the exposed glass to become etched during blasting. They apply easily to the surface of the glass and stick well during blasting. Equally important, they can be easily removed from the glass after blasting without leaving any adhesive residue behind.

Toughness

There are several important characteristics to consider in choosing a resist for a particular job. The toughness of the resist is a combination of the type of material used and the thickness of the material. The thicker the resist the better it can withstand the sandblast, but the more expensive it will be. *(The thickness is measured in mils. One mil is one thousandth of an inch.)*

Rubber based resists are the toughest available, but are usually only available in very thick layers *(40 mils thick or more)*, and consequently are very expensive. These resists are primarily used for very deep carving and are a waste of money for surface blasting.

Vinyl is tougher than polyethelyene, but not as tough as rubber. It is available down to 4 mils thick and is quite reasonable in cost. While a 4 mil vinyl is adequate for surface blasting, a 6 mil thick vinyl will give even better protection without increasing your cost significantly. On the other hand, using an 8 mil vinyl would be overkill and a waste of money.

Polyethylene is the least tough of the three, and requires a thicker layer than vinyl to give equal protection. For example, an 8 mil polyethylene is not quite as strong as a 6 mil vinyl. Polyethylene costs more than vinyl for an equal measure of protection, so if you were selecting resist by cost vs. protection alone you might think that polyethelyene would never be used. This couldn't be farther from the truth, however, based on the next characteristic of resists.

Ease of Transfer

This important characteristic is the ease of transfer of your pattern to the resist. For example, you have finalized your pattern on paper, you have applied the resist to the glass, and now you have to get the pattern on the resist before you can cut it out with your stencil knife. The vinyl and rubber resists are opaque, requiring you to take the time to manually transfer the pattern onto the resist. The polyetheylene resist is transparent, so you can completely eliminate this step. You simply place your design underneath a piece of clear glass covered with this resist. You can see through it well enough to cut out your design without transferring the design directly to the resist. This can save you a considerable amount of time, partially compensating for the higher cost of the clear polyethylene resist, however there are some disadvantages which are covered later in this chapter.

Type of Adhesives

The last important resist characteristic is the type of adhesive on the resist. It should be an adhesive that holds firmly to the glass during blasting, but releases easily when the resist is peeled from the glass after blasting. Some materials being sold as sandblast resists have adhesives that are almost permanent, and are very difficult to remove. In addition, the adhesive should not remain on the glass when the resist is peeled, it should be completely removed with the resist. Adhesives that remain on the glass can be quite time consuming and difficult to remove.

Alternate Resists

Other things can be used for resist, such as masking tape or duct tape. However, these are hard to apply to the glass and hard to remove once they are weakened by blasting. In addition, the force of the sandblaster may peel these off the glass while you are sandblasting, ruining your project. Self-adhesive vinyl shelf paper can also be used but has several limitations. This is a very thin vinyl material which is sometimes used for the lightest of surface blasting. Difficulties of this material are that it is so thin that the sandblaster can easily blast through any bubbles left in the material after you apply it to the glass. In addition, the adhesive tends to stay on the glass when you remove the material after blasting, particularly if you have left it on the glass more than a day. The adhesive can be quite difficult to remove and sometimes requires several applications of solvents such as acetone.

Applying the Resist

The resist has two layers, the actual resist material itself with adhesive backing, and a protective backing layer of waxed paper or plastic. You will need to cut a piece of resist about 1/2" larger all around than the glass you want to cover. To apply the resist, you peel about 1" of the backing layer back from the edge of the resist. Lay the resist down on the glass, making sure that the piece of resist completely covers the edges of the glass. Only when you are sure that the resist is aligned straight and square on the glass should you stick down the resist on the 1" exposed edge.

Mash the resist down firmly along the 1" exposed edge with your hand, squeezing out any air bubbles which may have been trapped under the resist. If you are right handed, you should start from the right side of the glass, holding the resist firmly in place with your left hand while you mash down the 1" exposed edge of the resist. *(When the 1" edge has been firmly adhered to the glass, the resist can't shift position.)* Then, reach in under the resist with your left hand and start peeling the backing layer out towards the left. As you are slowly peeling out the backing layer, mash the resist down firmly onto the glass with your right hand. On larger pieces of glass you will find it better to use a plastic squeegee to mash the resist down glass because the hard, flat surface of the squeegee helps prevent trapped air bubbles. Of course, you will want to reverse the above hand positions if you are left handed.

Continue until the resist completely covers the glass, then trim the edges of the resist back to the edges of the glass. Avoid trapping air bubbles under the resist because the sand can much more easily eat through the resist where there are bubbles. This is much more of a problem if you have a thin resist than one of 6 mils or thicker. If you have trapped air bubbles that will be close to the area you will be etching *(within 2" or so)*, you should gently puncture them with your stencil knife or a pin and squeeze the air out. If there is a visible hole left where you have punctured a bubble, cover it with a small piece of resist. You can ignore any bubbles more than 2" from any area of glass which will be etched if you can remember not to point the blaster directly at the bubbles while you are blasting. Going through this process once or twice will really sharpen your resolve to learn to apply the resist without bubbles.

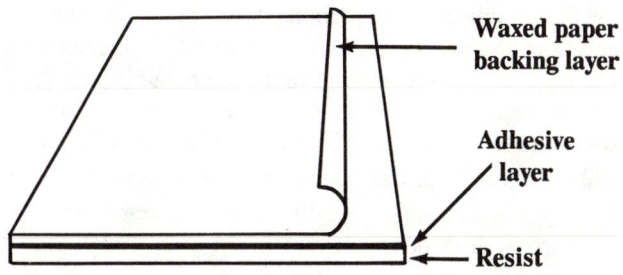

The waxed paper or plastic backing on the resist protects the adhesive on the resist, but is easily removed before applying the resist to the glass.

Peel the backing away from the resist about one inch down before adhering to the glass.

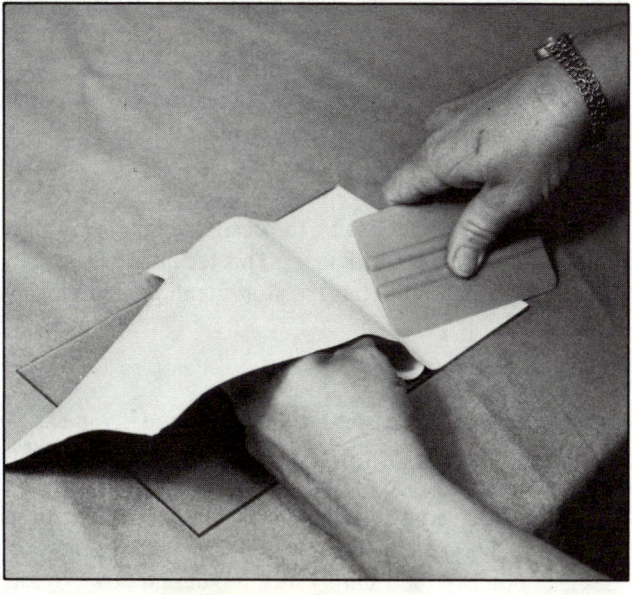

After the resist is adhered along one edge, slowly peel the backing out from underneath and squeegee the resist down on the glass.

Transferring the Design

The design must now be transferred to the resist prior to cutting with the stencil knife. If you have used the clear polyethylene resist, you can skip this step and simply place your design under the glass and it is ready to cut. Some people prefer using clear resist because it allows them to skip the transfer step. However, other people really don't like trying to cut the resist while looking through the glass at the design, because it is somewhat hard to see exactly where your cuts start and stop and it is hard to line up your cuts so that they match up properly. You should try this technique to see if you like it.

Carbon Paper or Graphite Paper

There are several ways to transfer your design to the opaque vinyl resist, with advantages and disadvantages to each. The most common way is to lay a sheet of carbon paper or graphite paper down on the resist, put the design down on the carbon paper or graphite paper and trace the design through to the resist. This does give you an accurate duplicate of your design, but it is time consuming. The image on the resist will smear easily if you touch it, but spraying it with an artist's spray fixative will keep that from happening. Fixative is available from art supply stores and is usually used to fix pencil drawings or charcoal drawings.

Graphite Transfer

A second way to transfer the design is called a graphite transfer. To do this properly, you have to have your original full sized drawing drawn with a very soft artist's pencil, a 4B or 6B. You then lay the original face down on the resist and rub hard on the back of the paper where the drawing is with a hard object like the back of your stencil knife. This will transfer the outline of the drawing onto the resist, but it won't be very dark and is even more delicate than the image from the carbon paper. Some vinyl resists take a graphite transfer better than others so try yours with a sample first. The rubber resists are much better with a graphite transfer. Remember that when you use this technique, the design on the resist will be the reverse of your original. This technique is faster than carbon paper, but has the aforementioned disadvantages.

Spray Adhesive

The next transfer technique is good if you can easily get multiple copies of your original design. Once again visiting the local art supply store, pick up a can of repositionable spray adhesive. Following the instructions on the can, spray the back of one of the copies of the design. You can then simply stick the design down to the resist and cut out the design with no time spent tracing at all. This can save you a lot of time, particularly if you are doing more than one etching with the same design, however there are some problems with this technique.

First, when you cut the pattern on the resist, you destroy the pattern, so it is essential to be able to get multiple copies inexpensively. Second, it is quite a bit more difficult to cut through the resist with the paper on top of it than it to cut the resist alone. A fresh stencil knife blade is essential. Then, when you have finished cutting out the design and have removed all areas of resist where you want to etch the glass, you still have to remove the rest of the paper from the resist. *(If you are using repositionable or temporary spray adhesive, this will be much easier than if you are using permanent spray adhesive.)* If you don't remove the paper that was left on the resist when the design was cut and peeled, it will become shredded when you blast it, potentially clogging up your blaster if you recycle your abrasive.

After trimming the resist to the edge of the glass, lay a piece of carbon paper on the resist, then the design on the carbon paper, then trace the design.

Cutting the Design

Once the resist is on the glass and the design is on the resist, you are ready to cut out the design. For this purpose, you will use a standard stencil knife, a stencil knife with a swivel blade or one of the new electric hot stencil cutters that is available at many stained glass shops. The standard knife is the most widely used. If you choose to use a swivel knife, get one of good quality because the cheap ones are practically useless. Also be prepared to practice quite a bit with the swivel knife to get used to it. When you do get used to it, it can really speed up cutting certain types of designs. The electric hot stencil cutters really don't replace standard knives, as they don't do straight lines as well and they don't work well with some types of vinyl resists. However some people swear by them for cutting small or irregular areas on a design. If you use the standard or swivel knives, have plenty of replacement blades available as the points break off easily.

Cut out each area to be etched with the stencil knife.

Using your chosen stencil cutter, cut around each area of the design which you want to be etched in the finished piece, and remove each separate area from the surface of the glass as it is cut. Try to make your cuts as clean as possible, leaving no ragged edges. The finished etching will be only as good as the stencil cutting and any irregular lines and ragged edges will definitely show.

When the whole design has been cut and all of the resist has been removed where you want the glass to be etched, check in all of the exposed areas of glass to make sure no adhesive remains from the resist. If there is adhesive, clean it off the glass before blasting as the adhesive will act as a resist for a few seconds before it is blasted off, causing the etched area to appear irregular or splotchy. If your design has a number of small lines of resist left on the glass, or if there are areas that may have been slightly pulled loose when you removed adjacent areas of resist, carefully mash down these areas again on the glass. This helps insure that the resist will stay on these areas when it is blasted.

As each area is cut, remove it from the glass.

All resist is removed from the areas to be etched.

13

Chapter 4
THE SANDBLASTING PROCESS

The next step is the actual blasting process, and interestingly enough it takes less time than any of the preparatory steps. You will be using one of the two types of sandblasters available, a siphon sandblaster or a pressure sandblaster, and you will probably be blasting in a blasting cabinet. Since the equipment will be discussed in detail in the next section, I'll only describe the process here.

Preparing to Sandblast

Be sure that the sandblaster is set for the proper pressure and that it is filled with sand or other abrasive. Set your piece of glass securely in position in the blasting cabinet so that the force of the blast will not cause it to fall and break. Adjust the lighting in the cabinet so that you can see what you are doing. Proper lighting is one of the most important considerations when blasting. It is difficult enough under the best conditions to adequately see what you are doing in the blasting cabinet, and without proper lighting it is impossible. You must be able to see properly or your finished etching will be uneven, splotchy and irregular.

The Blasting Process

When you are ready to blast, turn on the sandblaster and pass the nozzle of the blaster back and forth across the glass, holding the nozzle from four to six inches away from the glass. It is only necessary to blast the exposed areas of glass where the resist has been removed, overlapping onto the resist about 1/2" to insure even coverage. Start high on the glass and as you are passing the nozzle back and forth across the exposed glass, move the nozzle down a little more with each pass. Overlap the passes about 50% to get even coverage of the blast on the glass.

Blast the piece, being careful that all exposed areas of glass are evenly etched.

The glass on the left is ready to blast, the one on the right has been blasted.

Removing the resist from the blasted piece of glass.

After removing the resist, clean the piece and it is finished.

Below right:
The finished etching installed in a wood box.

Checking for Quality

After you finish blasting, take the glass out and wipe the dust off the front and back. Take a good, long critical look and check for irregularity of coverage. Make sure you have fully blasted all of the exposed areas. It is very easy to forget to fully blast very small areas and long narrow areas. If you find that some areas are irregular, mark across them with a felt tip marker and re-blast those areas. You will know when they are fully blasted when you blast away the lines from the marker.

Finishing Up

When you are satisfied that the blasting is completed remove the remaining resist from the surface of the glass and clean both sides of the glass. The piece is now finished and you can sit back to admire your work. If you are like most people, though, you will be so excited by your success that you won't take much time to admire your work before you are started on another piece!

Chapter 5
NOW WHAT CAN YOU MAKE?

The variety of things you can make that incorporate etched glass is almost endless. In fact the field is so wide that there are many possibilities that you might not discover on your own, so we decided to include a short chapter just to tell you about some of these possibilities. There are several broad categories to consider - items for home decorating, gifts, advertising and signs, commercial decorating, art works.

Home Decorating

Within the broad category of home decorating, the most obvious application of etching is in etched glass windows. These can be sidelight windows beside doors, windows in doors, kitchen windows, bathroom windows, living room picture windows. Anywhere there is a window you can etch the glass for it. In most cases you will want to leave the existing glass in place as protection for the etched glass, and mount a separate piece of etched glass behind it. This also will take care of the problem of tempered glass since the glass already installed in some of these locations will be tempered.

Other home decorating items you might not readily think of are glass shower and bath enclosures *(careful - probably tempered!)*, glass firescreens, glass table tops, glass shelves, cabinet doors, mirrors and mirrored closet doors. You can now get from many stained glass shops frames for screens, room dividers, coffee tables and end tables with glass tops. Some frame shops are now even etching the glass in picture frames!

Gifts

The category of gifts is even larger. Etched beveled glass pieces are particularly attractive, whether done individually as small gifts or incorporated into full scale beveled windows. If you do stained glass work, you can make lampshades with etched accents and jewelry boxes with etched tops and sides. Etched hand mirrors can be elegant. Etched Christmas ornaments of flashed glass or mirror are striking. There is a whole subcategory of glassware that you can etch, such as wine glasses, beer mugs, serving trays, plates, bowls, crystal ice buckets - the list is endless! Monograms, names and logos are particularly in demand etched on glassware.

Stained Glass Windows

Etched detail in stained glass windows can lend a delicacy and intricacy that would be impossible to achieve any other way. You can use this technique to create veins in flower petals and leaves, for example.

Wood Accessories

There are some great wood accessories now on the market which have been designed to be used with stained glass gift projects but which are also excellent with etched glass. For example, pencil and pen sets, bookends, and wood boxes with glass tops.

Signs

There is a big market now in etched glass signs because the signs will never fade or peel as will painted signs. Most of these are interior signs since there is a much greater chance of breakage with a glass sign outside.

Commercial Uses

The commercial decorating field includes glass booth dividers in restaurants, room dividers, windows *(interior and exterior)*, table tops, bar mirrors and more. Advertising specialties with business names and logos include ashtrays, coasters, pencil and pen sets, and paperweights.

Art Glass

The art glass field includes many of the above mentioned products plus free standing sculptural pieces, and also many possibilities in etching fused and slumped glass.

The number of things you can etch is limited only by your imagination. There is even demand now for etching from owners of custom cars, vans and motor homes, not to mention large yachts and sailboats.

Before you can do any etching though, you need to understand some things about etching equipment and safety procedures when etching, and that is the subject of the next section of this book.

SECTION II
GLASS ETCHING EQUIPMENT and SAFETY PROCEDURES

If you don't own the proper equipment for sandblast glass etching, and don't intend to purchase any soon, there are many stained glass shops and studios that will rent you their equipment to use on your etching projects. The rental prices are usually quite reasonable considering how much etching you can do in a short time.

When you do decide to purchase your own equipment, it will be very important to understand the following chapters because it may save you considerable expense in purchasing the right equipment for your needs. Even if you plan to rent equipment, it will be to your advantage to read on. Understanding the equipment necessary to do a craft is essential to becoming good at it and to expanding your skills. Either way, you should definitely read the chapter on safety.

Chapter 6
COMPRESSORS

An air compressor is a machine that is the source of compressed air which runs the sandblaster. The smallest compressor that is adequate to power most sandblasters would be a two horsepower model that puts out at least 6 CFM at 100 PSI. Those ratings represent the power of the compressor motor and the volume of air it will produce at a given pressure. Most 2 HP compressors come wired for 230 volt electricity, but can be easily re-wired in about ten minutes for 115 volt household

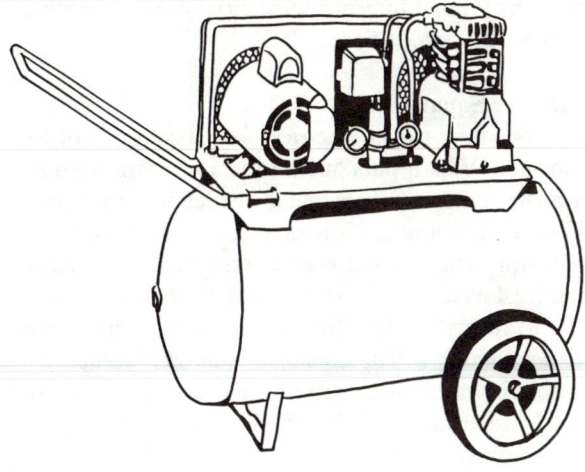

2 HP portable compressor with 20 gallon tank.

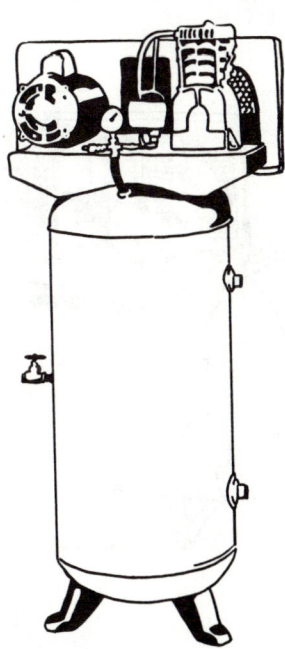

Stationary 4 HP compressor with 30 gallon tank.

current. Have an electrician or your compressor dealer do it for you if you don't feel confident following the instructions yourself. If you do have it re-wired, it will require at least a 20 amp circuit to plug it into, so make sure *(by checking your circuit breaker or fuse)* that the circuit you plan to plug it into can handle the load. To check the exact amperage required for your particular compressor, consult the specification plate on the motor of your compressor.

If the foregoing paragraph sounds like Greek to you, or if you want more than just the most basic summary of compressor requirements, please continue reading for a more detaned explanation. If you take the time to learn a little more, you could save yourself a lot of money in the long run.

Electrical Requirements for Compressors

Air compressors are powered by electricity or by gasoline. *(For now, we will just consider the electric compressors.)* The electricity required depends on how large the compressor is, but in most cases it will either be 115 volt household current or 230 volt current for heavy duty motors. Most of the outlets in your house are 115 volt. 230 volt is used primarily for electric stoves and electric clothes dryers.

Single Phase vs. Three Phase

Both 115 and 230 volt electrical currents are called single phase. This is the type of electricity that is available everywhere. You may run across compressors which require three phase electricity. That is a type of electricity which is available only in industrial areas. You can't use these compressors unless you have three phase power in your area. Even if you do have three phase where you are now, if you ever move you may not have it in your new location. It is also much harder to sell a three phase compressor since so few people can use them. For those reasons it is usually wise to avoid three phase compressors, even if they are substantially less expensive to operate than single phase.

Pressure Per Square Inch

You have to put electricity into a compressor to get it to run. What it puts out in return is compressed air and it is the compressed air that is needed to power your sandblaster. The amount, or volume, of compressed air that a compressor puts out is important because it needs to be at least as much as your particular sandblaster needs in order to run properly. *(How to tell the air requirements of your sandblaster will be explained in the next section.)* The amount of air that a compressor puts out is measured in cubic feet per minute or CFM. The CFM that a particular compressor puts out is different at different air pressures, so in comparing compressors it is necessary to compare them at the same air pressure. This pressure is measured in pounds per square inch or PSI for short. For example, a compressor that puts out 6 CFM at 100 PSI will put out about 7 CFM at 50 PSI.

Horsepower

The only measure of compressor size that most people are familiar with is the horsepower rating of the motor. This is a valid piece of information to know but you can't make a decision about buying a compressor based solely on the horsepower. The reason for this is that there are different levels of quality of compressors, unofficially designated as consumer, commercial, and industrial qualities. An industrial quality 5 HP compressor puts out about twice the CFM of air that is produced by a consumer quality 5 HP compressor, and costs more than twice as much. In addition to producing more CFM of air per horsepower, the better quality compressors will last much longer and will cost less per year for maintenance. So you can't just go out looking for a 5 HP compressor and buy the cheapest one you can find. You get what you pay for in compressors more than almost anything else, so a cheap 5 HP compressor may be completely inadequate for your particular situation.

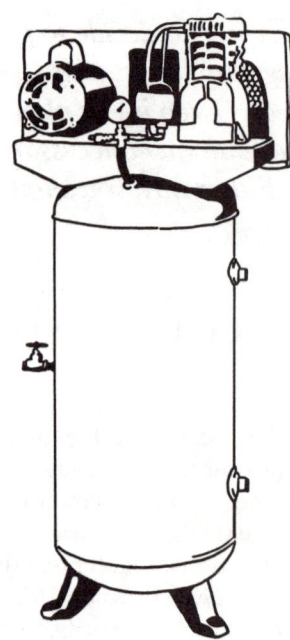

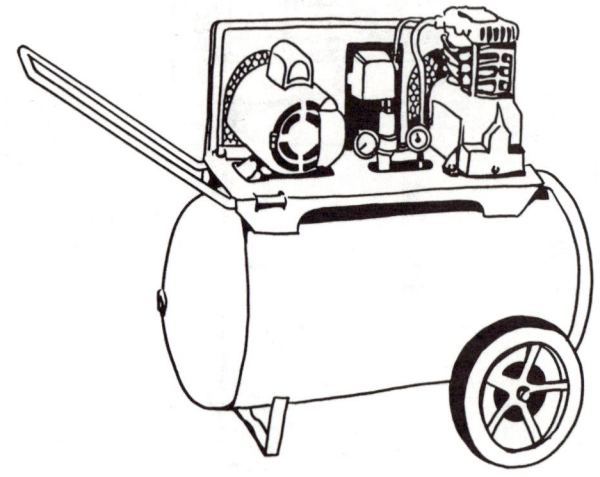

Single and Two-Stage Compressors

You may also hear the terms *single stage* and *two stage* when discussing compressors. A single stage compressor has only one size of piston, and produces air pressure only up to 120 PSI. A two stage compressor has two different piston sizes. The large piston compresses the air to 120 PSI and a smaller piston which takes the 120 PSI air and compresses it even further up to about 175 PSI. Since the maximum air pressure you are ever likely to use in glass etching is around 100 to 110 PSI, the extra pressure you get from a two stage compressor is of no value. In general, two stage compressors are commercial or industrial quality, so you may get one simply by opting for a higher quality compressor.

The Air Tank

There is one last component of a compressor that needs to be mentioned and that is the air tank. The air tank stores a certain amount of the compressed air produced by the compressor. This storage capacity keeps the compressor from running constantly when you are using air. Air is used from the storage tank first and when that air is depleted, the compressor turns on automatically, building up the air in the tank again, before turning off. The tank size is not a significant factor in choosing a compressor as long as it is at least 20 gallons. A larger tank allows the compressor's off cycle to be longer than it would be if the tank were smaller, but by the same token, the on cycle is also longer. This provides very little difference in electrical consumption and compressor wear and tear.

Gasoline Compressors

Gasoline compressors work very much like electric compressors except that they have gas engines rather than electric motors. Gas compressors are usually only used when no electricity is available where the compressor is located. Gas compressors are more expensive but much less efficient than electric compressors. For example, it takes a 5 HP gas compressor to put out the same CFM that a 3 HP electric compressor puts out. Gas compressors are also noisier, put out noxious exhaust fumes, and are much more expensive to operate and to maintain than electric compressors. For these reasons, we recommend that you avoid gas compressors.

In order to determine the best compressor for your sandblasting needs, we now need to move on to the section on sandblasters. Since the compressor and sandblaster work hand in hand, they need to be matched as well as possible.

Chapter 7
SANDBLASTERS AND ABRASIVES

Sandblasters

The size of compressor you need for best results can vary considerably with the sandblaster that you are using. There are two basic types of sandblasters made today, the siphon system and the pressure system.

Siphon System

The siphon system is the cheapest but most inefficient, and requires a much larger compressor to do adequate work. The siphon system consists of a sandblast gun with a trigger mechanism or foot pedal, an open hopper made of sheet metal or plastic to hold the abrasive, and an abrasive hose connecting the gun with the hopper. *(see illustration)* To blast, you fill the hopper, connect the air hose from the compressor to the gun and pull the trigger.

When the trigger is pulled, compressed air rushes through the gun and out the nozzle. As it goes through the gun, it passes over the inlet of the abrasive hose, picking up *(siphoning)* particles of abrasive and propelling them out the nozzle. In order to be effective, the air pressure required for a siphon system is 80 to 110 PSI.

Pressure System

The pressure system is a more sophisticated but more expensive piece of equipment which enables you to blast much faster than the siphon system while at the same time using much less air from the compressor. The pressure system is about four times faster at 40 PSI than the siphon system is at 100 PSI. This allows you to use about 50% less CFM from the compressor, which means you can either use a smaller compressor or that you will have less wear and tear on a larger compressor.

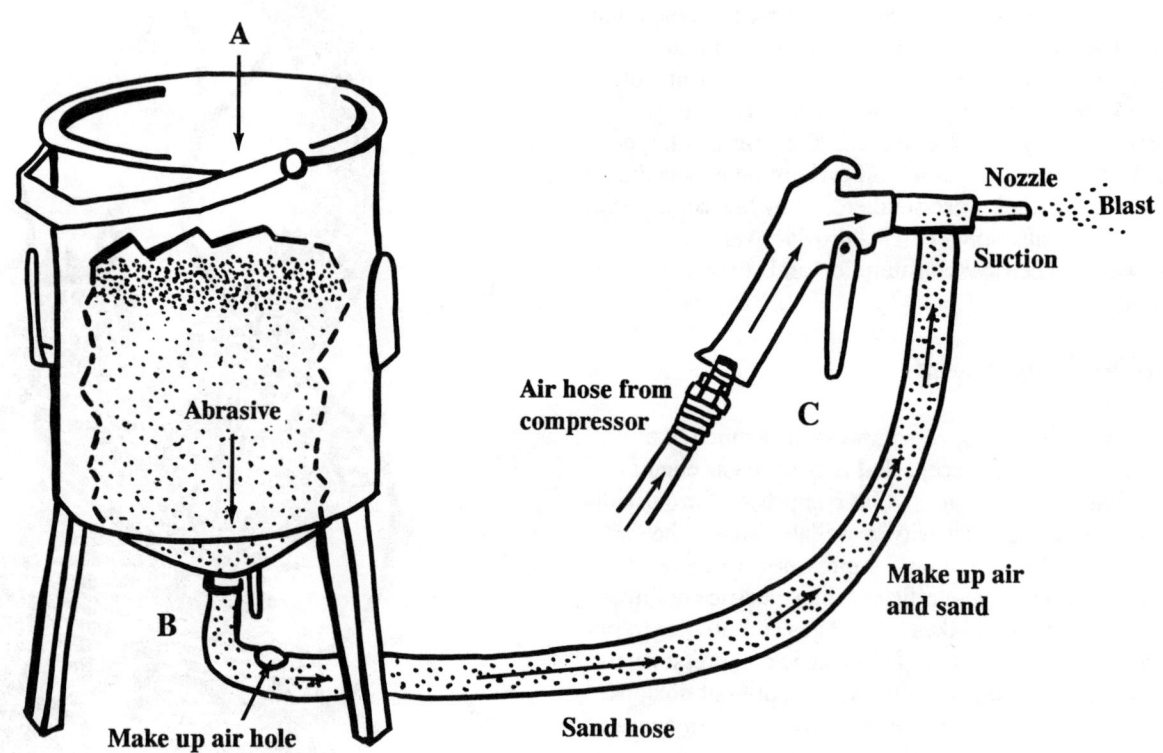

HOW A SIPHON SANDBLASTER WORKS

A. *The open hopper is filled with abrasive.*

B. *The abrasive drops through the funnel in the bottom of the hopper into the sand hose. Make up air, entering the sand hose from a small hole on top of the hose, mixes with the abrasive and allows it to move more evenly through the hose.*

C. *When the trigger on the gun is squeezed, compressed air flows through the gun, picking up bits of abrasive from the sand hose inlet and propelling them out the nozzle. The suction that is created by the air passing through the nozzle continuously siphons abrasive up through the sand hose.*

This system is called a pressure system because the hopper which contains the sand is under pressure, and it is not in the siphon system. Since it is under pressure, it must be made of heavy gauge steel, welded and pressure tested. The reason for pressurizing the sand tank is that feeding the sand into the air stream under pressure is much more efficient than feeding it into the air stream via the suction principle of the siphon system. This higher efficiency is the reason for the increased speed of the pressure system and the decreased air consumption.

In addition to higher speed and efficiency, with the pressure system you have the ability to regulate the exact flow of sand from very light to very heavy, giving you the ability to create different effects much more easily. While this sand regulation won't be used extensively in surface etching, it will be in the techniques of carving and shading.

The pressure system consists of the pressurized sand tank, a heavy duty hose which carries the sand/air mixture from the tank to the nozzle, and the nozzle assembly which is usually an on/off valve, the nozzle holder and nozzle. Properly set up, pressure systems also have pressure regulators and water separators, for most efficient operation.

While the pressure systems are somewhat more complicated and more expensive than are siphon systems, their increased speed and versatility more than compensate for those disadvantages.

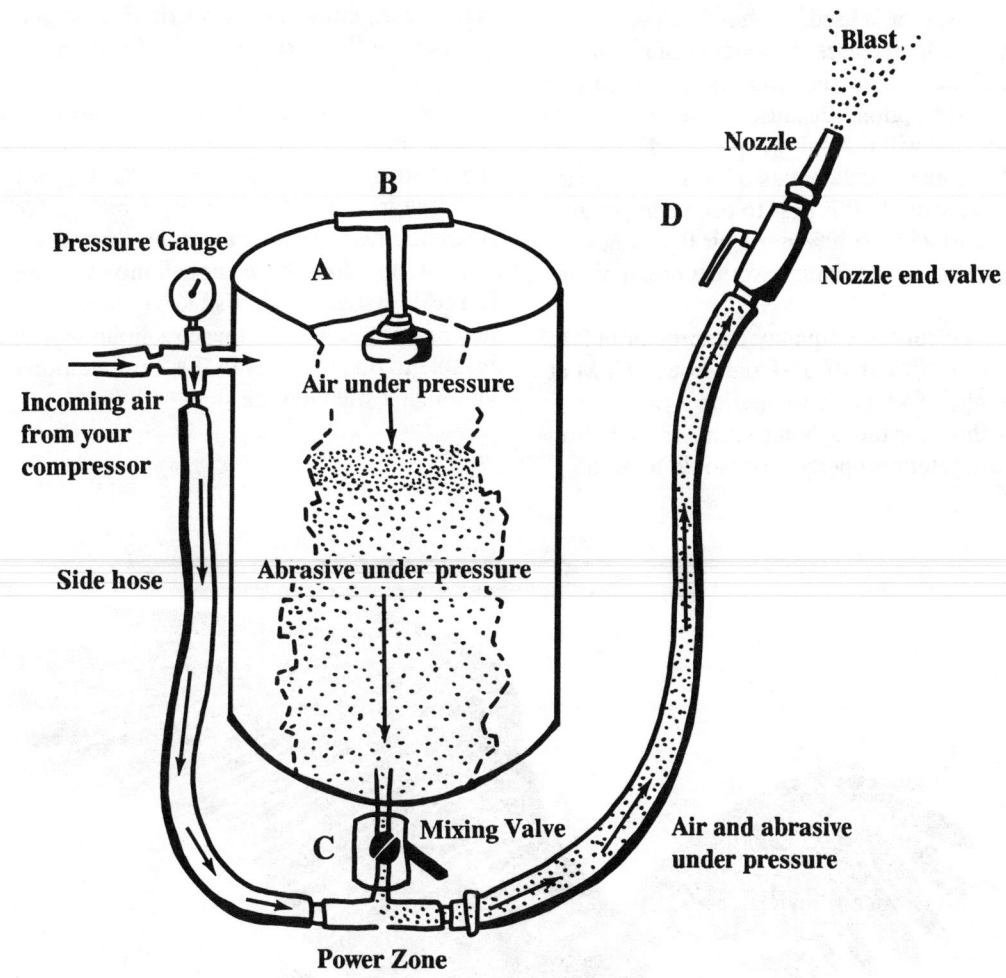

HOW A PRESSURE SANDBLASTER WORKS

A. The sealed top of the pressure tank is opened and abrasive is poured into the tank through the funnel at the top.

B. The top is pulled shut and the tank is pressurized with the incoming air from the compressor. The desired blasting pressure is set with the regulator (not shown).

C. Adjustment is made for the correct amount of abrasive with the mixing valve at the bottom of the tank. The abrasive flows into the compressed air stream in the "power zone", under the tank.

D. The nozzle end valve is opened, which permits the sand/air mixture to be propelled out the nozzle under great force.

Determining Air Requirements

With either type of sandblast system, the amount of air required to run it is based on two things, the nozzle size and the pressure at which the blaster will be used. The smallest nozzle size commonly available or pressure blasters is 3/32" and the average highest pressure at which the pressure blasters are used for glass is about 40 to 50 PSI. Set up this way, a pressure system will use about 5.5 CFM of air from the compressor.

Since the siphon blasters are less efficient, the smallest commonly available nozzle size is 3/16" and the average highest pressure that would be used for glass would be 100 to 110 PSI. With these conditions, the siphon blaster will use about 12 CFM of air.

As either blaster is used, the nozzle slowly enlarges in size, which increases the amount of air used. With only a small increase in diameter, there is a dramatic increase in air comsumption. Because of this, it is wise to get a compressor that will not only supply an adequate amount of air for a new nozzle but also for a nozzle that has been moderately used. It is best to get a compressor that puts out at least 25% to 50% more air than a new nozzle will require at the maximum average pressure.

An average consumer quality compressor of 2 HP will put out about 6 CFM at 100 PSI and about 7 CFM at 50 PSI. This would be adequate to operate a pressure system but falls short for the siphon system. In order to power the siphon system properly, you would have to move up to a commercial quality 5 HP compressor, producing about 16 CFM at 100 PSI. It only takes a little research to find out that a pressure system and a 2 HP compressor cost the same or less than a siphon system and a 5 HP commercial compressor.

When you have a compressor that will not produce as much air as your blaster uses, what happens is that after five, ten or fifteen minutes of blasting, the compressor runs out of air and you have to stop blasting. You then wait for the compressor to build the pressure back up again so you can resume blasting. After three or four cycles of this, the compressor has been running continuously for 30 to 45 minutes and is beginning to overheat. You should now stop blasting long enough for the compressor to cool down or damage to the compressor may occur. Constantly waiting for the compressor to catch up is time consuming and very irritating, so get an adequate compressor if you can possibly afford one.

One last thing to keep in mind is that the above figures for air consumption are based on continuous use of the blasters. Also keep in mind that beginning glass etchers rarely use a blaster continuously, hour after hour. If you are just starting out, don't mind waiting for the compressor, and don't have enough money in the budget for a full scale system, it is possible to use a small compressor like one of 2 HP and a low cost siphon system. You will be able to do etching with this combination of equipment, although it will be quite slow.

Abrasives

Sand is considered by some to be the only or primary abrasive used for sandblasting. Don't be fooled by the name "sandblasting"! There are several abrasives that are much better for blasting glass than sand is. There are two main drawbacks to using sand. First sand is relatively slow in etching glass and it can't be effectively re-used more than once or twice. Abrasive particles are more effective the sharper they are and the sand particles get smooth and rounded very quickly when they are re-used so they lose their effectiveness.

Health considerations provide the second reason that sand is not good to use. Sand, like glass, is composed mostly of silica. Sandblasting with sand breaks down the sand particles into a fine dust that is, chemically speaking, free silica. Free silica, breathed in large enough quantities over time can cause silicosis which is a fatal lung disease. If you do blast with sand, be sure to take the utmost in safety precautions *(see chapter 9)*. The insidious thing about silicosis is that it takes some time to build up and when you finally find out you have it, it is too late.
The only positive thing about using sand is that it is cheap. If you are blasting outside and have no way of recovering your abrasive and re-using it, you may have to use sand. If you are blasting in a cabinet or in a blast room where you can recover the abrasive *(see chapter 8)*, there is no excuse for using sand.

Some other abrasives that are used for etching glass are garnet, aluminum oxide and silicon carbide. **Garnet** can be recycled a few more times than sand can, and is usually 4 to 8 times more expensive.

Aluminum oxide can be recycled indefinitely because the particles do not wear down smooth like sand and garnet do. As the particles are used over and over, they break down into smaller and smaller pieces, but they break along cleavage planes, always maintaining their sharpness. Eventually the particles become small enough that they will be sucked out of a blasting cabinet by the exhaust system as dust, so you will need to replenish your supply from time to time.

Aluminum oxide is 15 to 20 times more expensive than sand but is much cheaper in the long run since you can re-use it so many times. It is also much faster than sand when used for etching glass. The disadvantage to aluminum oxide is that it tends to generate a lot of static electricity and that causes it to cling to the opposite side of the glass you are blasting. Since you need to see through your glass in many cases to see if your etching is even, you have to constantly be wiping the dust off the back of the glass.

Silicon carbide is considered to be the best of all the abrasives for etching glass. It has all the advantages of aluminum oxide but does not genterate nearly as much static electricity. In addition, it displays what is called the flashlight effect when you are blasting. That is, when you are blasting, the particles of carbide hitting the glass create tiny sparks. Thousands of tiny sparks all together look like a tiny flashlight beam on the glass right where you are blasting. That way you can always tell just where your nozzle is pointing, allowing you to get an even etch on the glass without wasting time going over areas that are already etched. Silicon carbide is 25 to 30 times more expensive than sand, but the advantages far outweigh the cost. The carbide can be re-cycled over 100 times, making the cost per cycle actually much less than sand.

The primary disadvantage to both the carbide and the oxide is their expense. The only way they are practical is if you can recapture and recycle them to get the full use out of them.

Glass Beads are sometimes advertised as a sandblasting abrasive. These are practically useless for etching glass as they are like very well used, worn out sand particles. Glass beads are used to remove rust, corrosion or other unwanted deposits from metals without harming the metal surface.

23

Chapter 8
BLASTING CABINETS

The last basic requirement for blasting is a place to blast. When you are just starting and have a limited budget, you may have to blast outside. People have been known to take their glass out and lean it up against their house or garage and blast away.

While this will do in a pinch, it is not the most pleasant thing to do in the dead of winter during a snowstorm or midday on a summer day in the sun with the temperature at 100 degrees. Rain, wind, sleet and a few other weather conditions may be somewhat uncomfortable for the outside-behind-the-garage glass etcher. But, if you still want to do it that way, don't forget to wear your safety gear *(see chapter 9)* and don't forget to cover the wall behind your glass with a heavy plastic dropcloth. The same blaster that etches your glass will definitely take the paint off of your house. If all this still fails to deter you from wanting to blast outside, just wait till the pile of sand starts to build up and the neighborhood cats find it!

If all these cautions sound like they could possibly have been learned the hard way, you're right. Of course, when I learned them, I didn't have the money to buy a good blasting cabinet, or the knowledge to build one. When I got good and tired of the cats, I finally built a blasting cabinet and put it into my studio. Of course, I had built it all wrong so it leaked sand like a sieve. It was a little too short for me, and I was always blasting hunchbacked, which was pretty uncomfortable although my chiropracter thought it was great. *(I traded him a lot of etched glass for working on my back.)*

I finally gave up and bought a manufactured blasting cabinet and the first time I used it, I kicked myself for not getting one sooner. A good quality, well engineered sandblasting cabinet can actually make glass etching an enjoyable hobby. The cabinet will have a wide door to allow you to put a large piece of glass inside and a window to allow you to see what you are doing without either getting blasted in the face or having to wear a face shield. It has a pair of arm holes with gloves in them to allow you to hold your glass and the blast nozzle without blasting your hands, arms, watch and rings. An interior light illuminates your work.

The cabinet has a hopper in the bottom to catch the spent abrasive so it can easily be cleaned out, and last but not least it has a vacuum exhaust system. The exhaust system keeps the dust sucked out of the cabinet so you can see what you are doing and so you will have less chance of breathing the dust. There must be an auxiliary air inlet in conjunction with the exhaust system for it to work properly.

The only disadvantage with a blasting cabinet is that it won't hold a piece of glass that is bigger that it is. Cabinets that are 2' by 3' are common but get a 2' by 4' size if you can. It is more expensive but will hold most of the glass you will want to etch. Of course, there will be times when you want to etch a piece of glass that just happens to be four feet and one inch long, and for most people that means a trip back to the old sand pile out back.

If you are lucky, you will have space to build a sandblast room. A properly designed sandblast room will have an adjustable easel to put any size glass on, adjustable back and front lighting for the glass, a floor that is easily cleaned of abrasive, and it will be well sealed. It will also have a much more powerful vacuum exhaust system than a cabinet does. Although construction of a blasting room is beyond the scope of this book, they are certainly nice to have if you can afford one and have the proper safety gear.

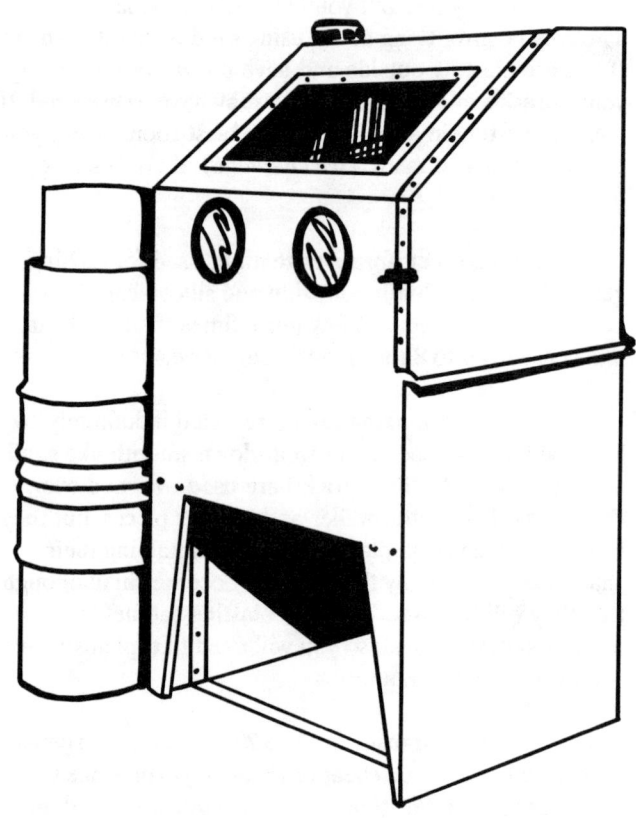

Features of a good quality manufactured sandblast cabinet include a vacuum exhaust system, a wide viewing window, rubber gloves, an overhead light, and a fully opening door.

Chapter 9
SAFETY EQUIPMENT

You need safety equipment while sandblasting to protect your eyes and skin from the effects of the abrasive and to protect your lungs from the dust that is generated.

Protection for Your Head and Neck

If you are blasting outside or in a blast room, you should always wear a hood designed for sandblasting. This will protect your head, face, eyes and neck from the reflected particles of abrasive. If you are blasting in a cabinet, the window in the cabinet will protect you and you can eliminate the headgear.

Rubber gloves will protect your hands and arms, especially if you hold the glass that you are blasting rather than setting it on an easel. If you blast in a cabinet, gloves will be a feature included in the cabinet.

Protection for Your Lungs

Protecting your lungs from the dust is the most difficult thing to do. If you blast in a cabinet, this is easier because a commercial cabinet should include a vacuum exhaust system the keeps your dust exposure level to a minimum. It is still wise to wear a good quality, dual filter passive respirator while blasting in a cabinet because you will be exposed to the dust when you open the cabinet, when you refill your blaster, and when you clean off your glass after blasting. You should definitely use a respirator if you are using sand as an abrasive. In picking a respirator, make sure it has filters approved for dust and mist. There are many different filters available, many of which are inadequate for sandblasting.

Dual filter passive respirator with head carriage suspension.

If you are blasting outside on a very intermittent basis, a good passive respirator may be adequate since there is usually enough air movement to carry the dust away from you. However, if you are blasting outside on a regular basis or in a blast room, you need an air supplied hood and respirator system. This is especially true if you are using sand. These systems can be purchased to be used with your existing compressor, if it is large enough to power your blaster and your hood at the same time *(at least a large 5 HP model)*.

By far the best system is to use a separate air pump to supply air to the hood. These air pumps are especially made to supply breathing air and meet stringent government regulations. In addition to being very safe, this system does not use air from your compressor, and is no more expensive in the long run.

Protection for Your Ears

The last safety consideration, and one that is generally overlooked, is protecting your ears. Sandblasters make a loud, high pitched sound when in use, and some compressors are also quite loud. If you blast on a reqular basis, you would be wise to wear hearing protection.

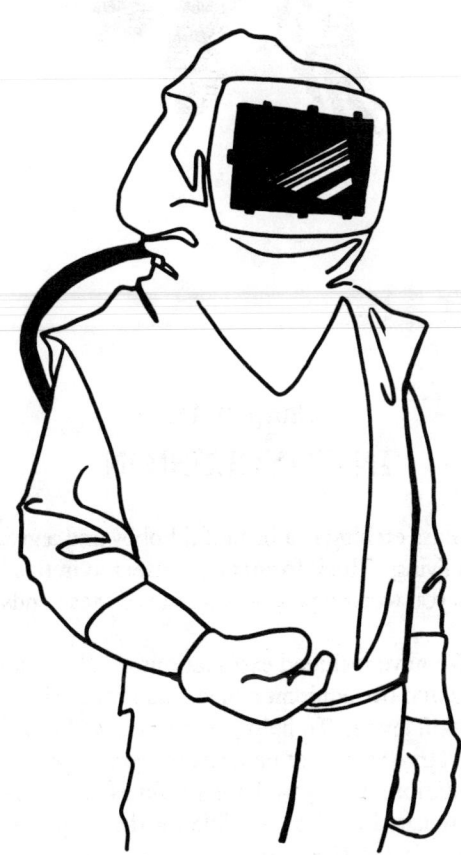

An air-supplied hood system provides maximum safety.

25

Chapter 10
IN CONCLUSION

Glass etching is a beautiful hobby and a great way to make a living. The information presented in this book should get you well on your way to one of these ends.

We have included explanations of all the basic techniques and the equipment necessary for projects of all sizes and skill levels. To help you further, we have included a large variety of patterns for your own use and experimentation. Lastly we have shown as many color photos of finished work as possible for the purposes of example and instruction. Hopefully this will all serve our goal: for you to find pleasure and success in your glass etching experiences.

Once you have learned surface etching and have explored some of its potential, you will undoubtedly want to learn the more advanced techniques of carving and shading. These techniques will give further realism and sophistication to your etching, but they take more time to master. We are now working on book two which will be all about carving on glass with the sandblaster, and a third book about shading is in the planning stages.

We wish you well with your etching and encourage you to go on learning all you can about surface etching and the other forms of glass etching.

SECTION III
DESIGNS FOR ETCHING

The design section of this book has been planned to give a good variety of subject matter, historical design styles, and degree of complexity. Look at each one with a creative eye and consider various ways in which they could be used. Many are designed to fit nicely on a single bevel. Two or more could possibly be combined in one larger etched piece. Also consider using just a section of one as your complete design, perhaps with a border added.

Most of the designs are presented full-size. Several of the more complex ones are ideal for enlarging to a sidelight size and are available individually in full-size pattern form. Please see page 96 for information on these.

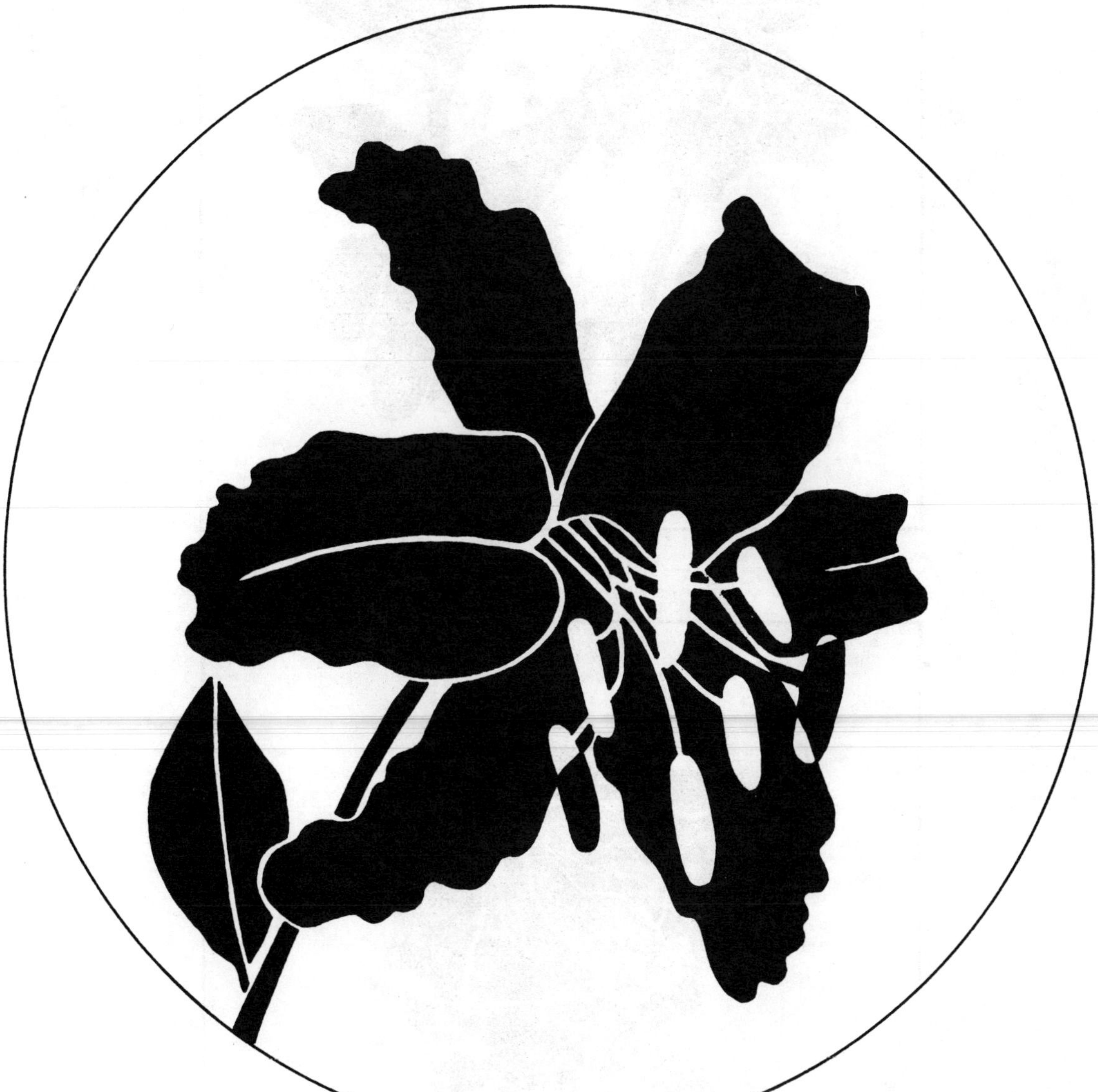

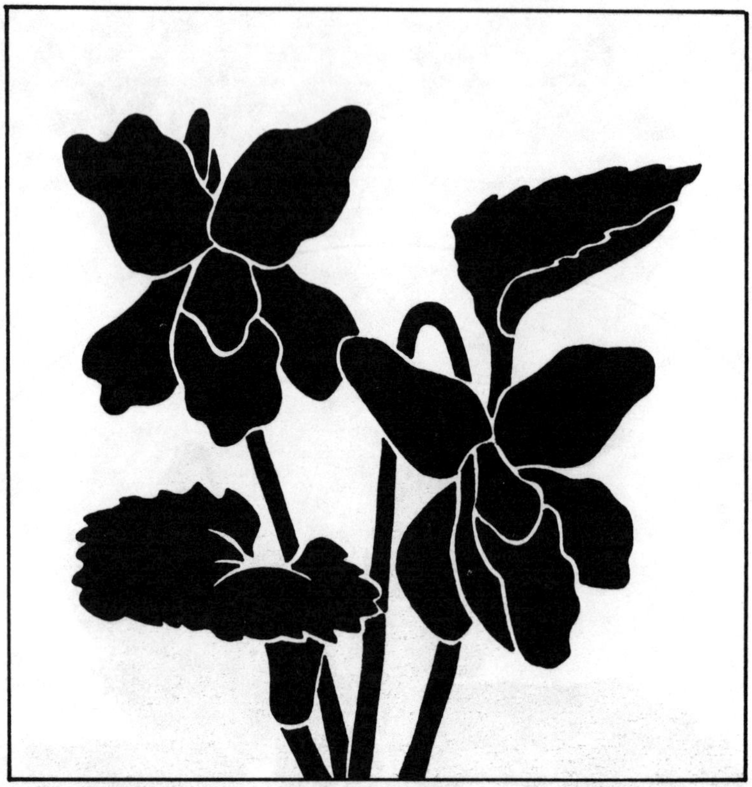

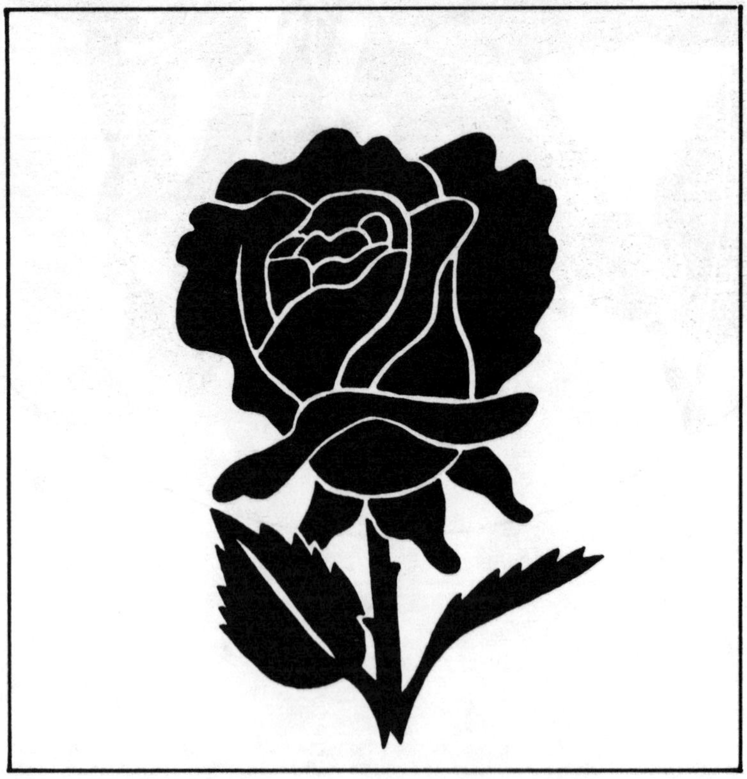

31

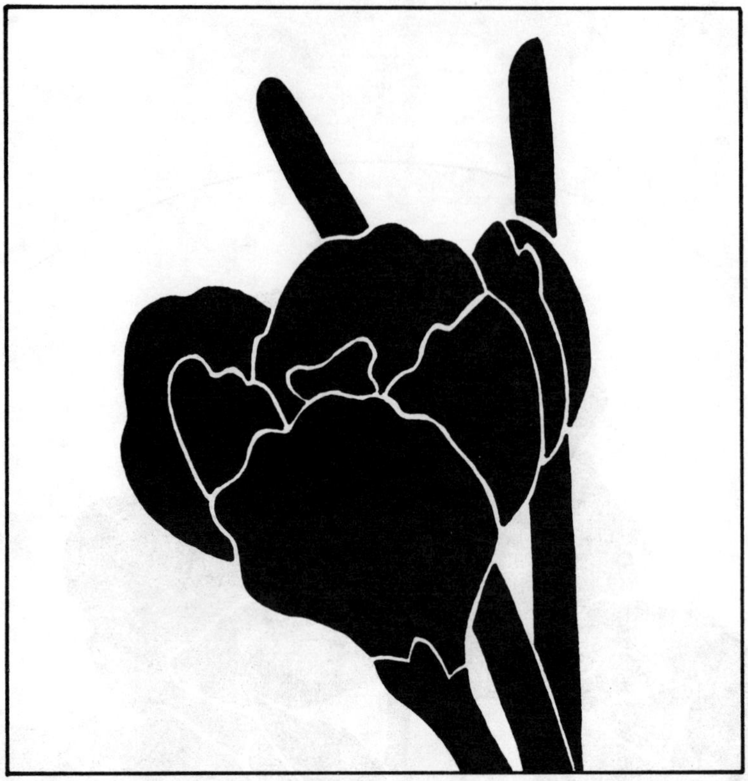

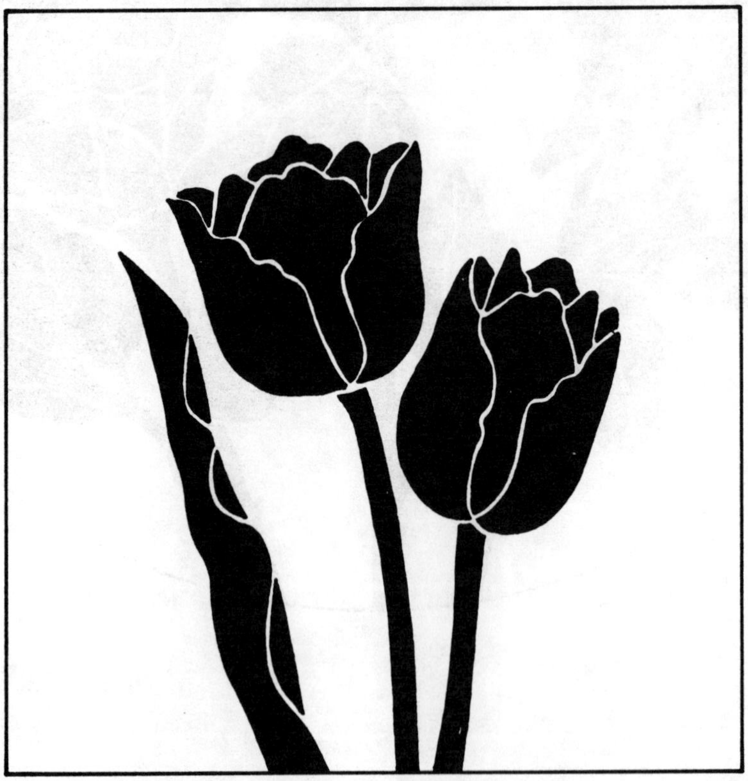

33

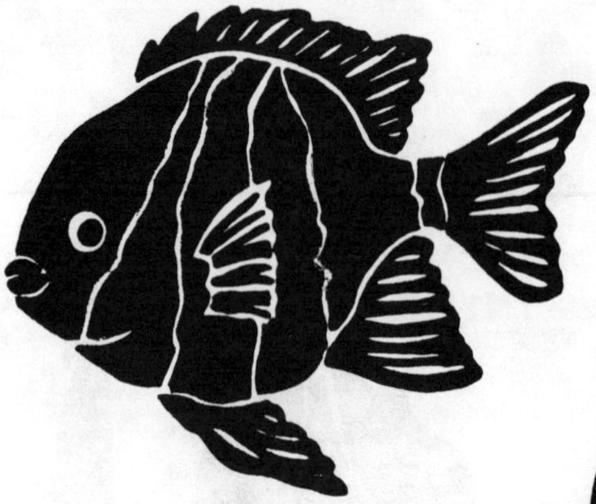
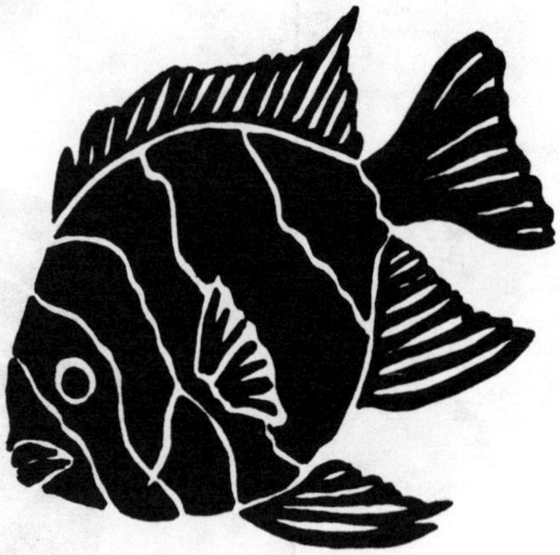
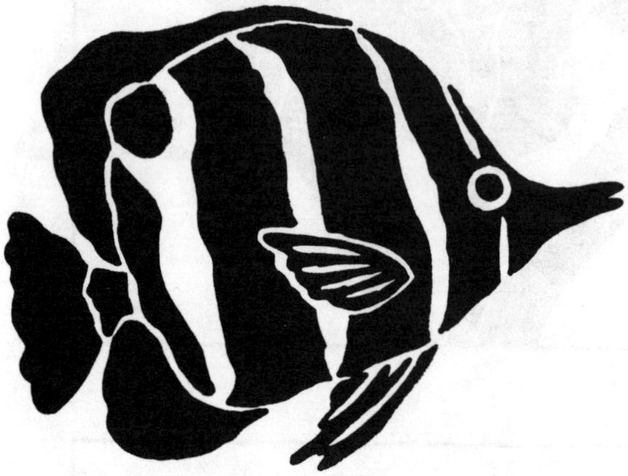
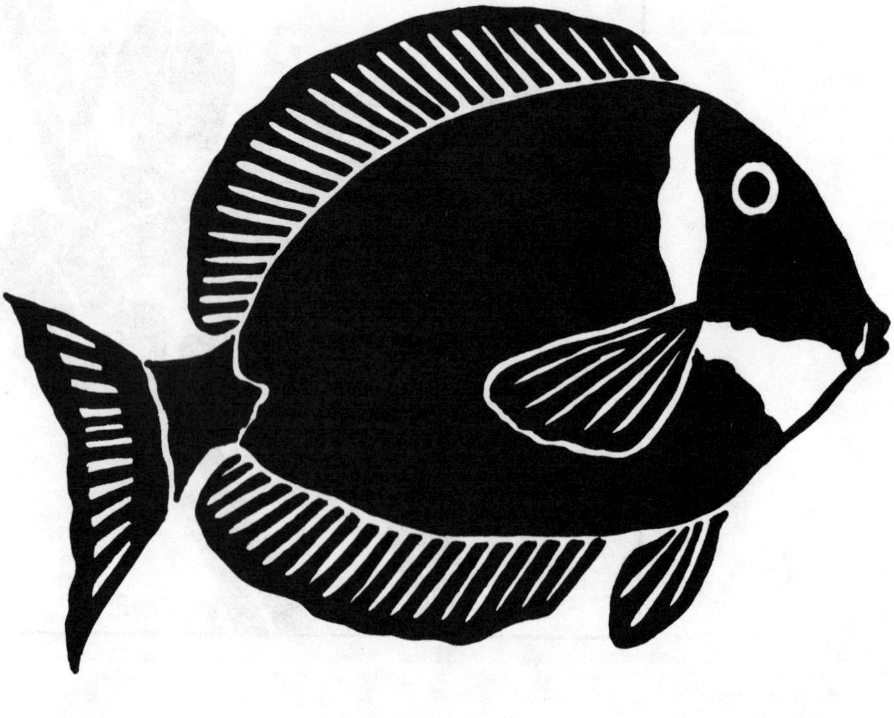

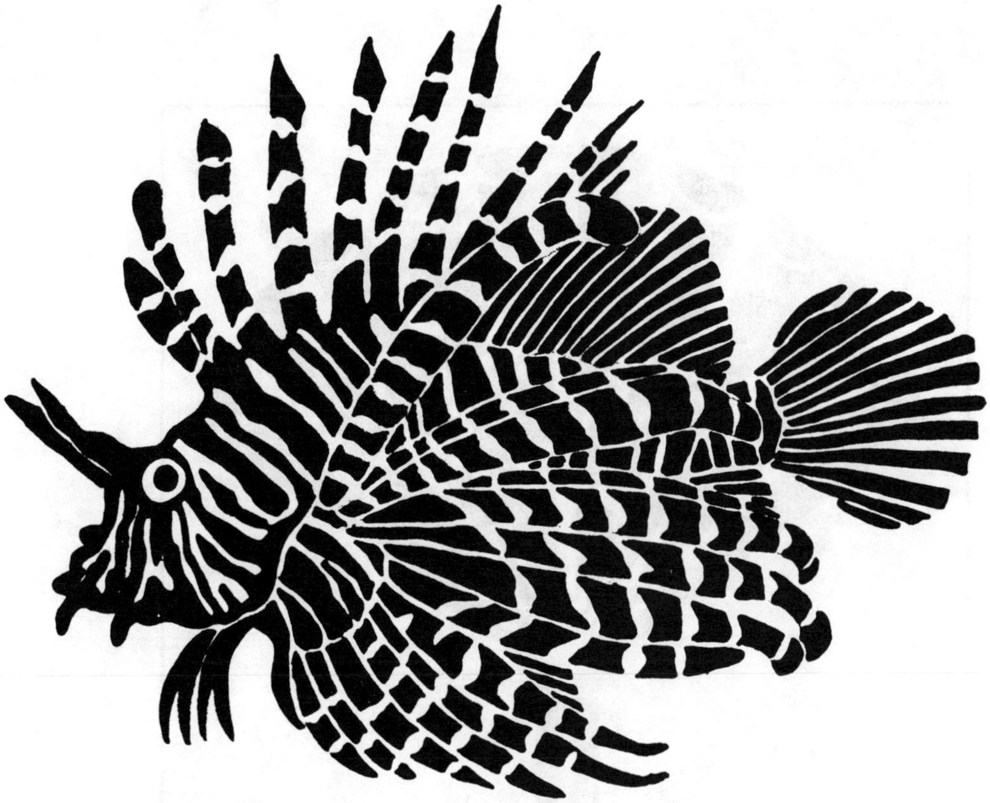

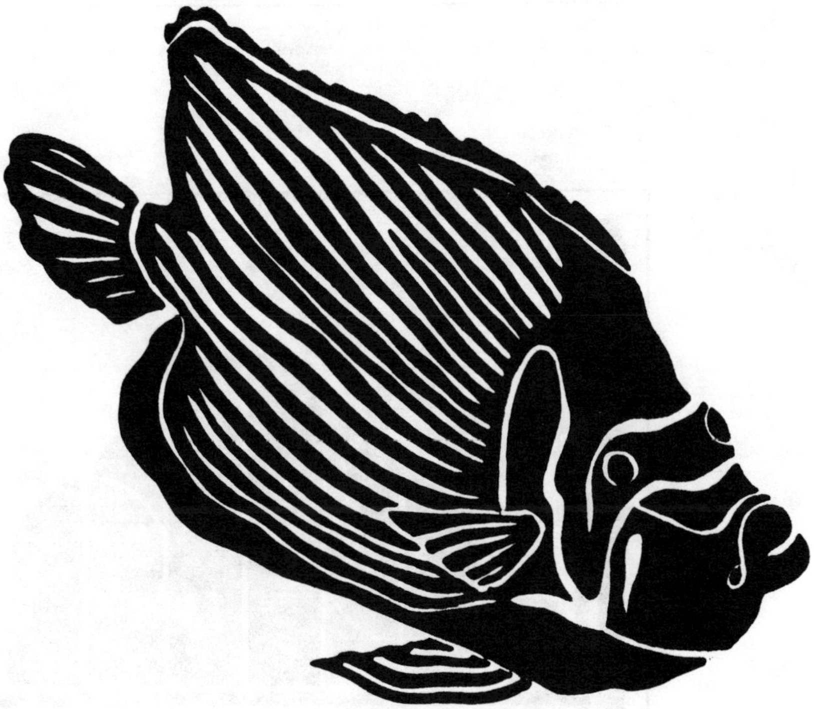

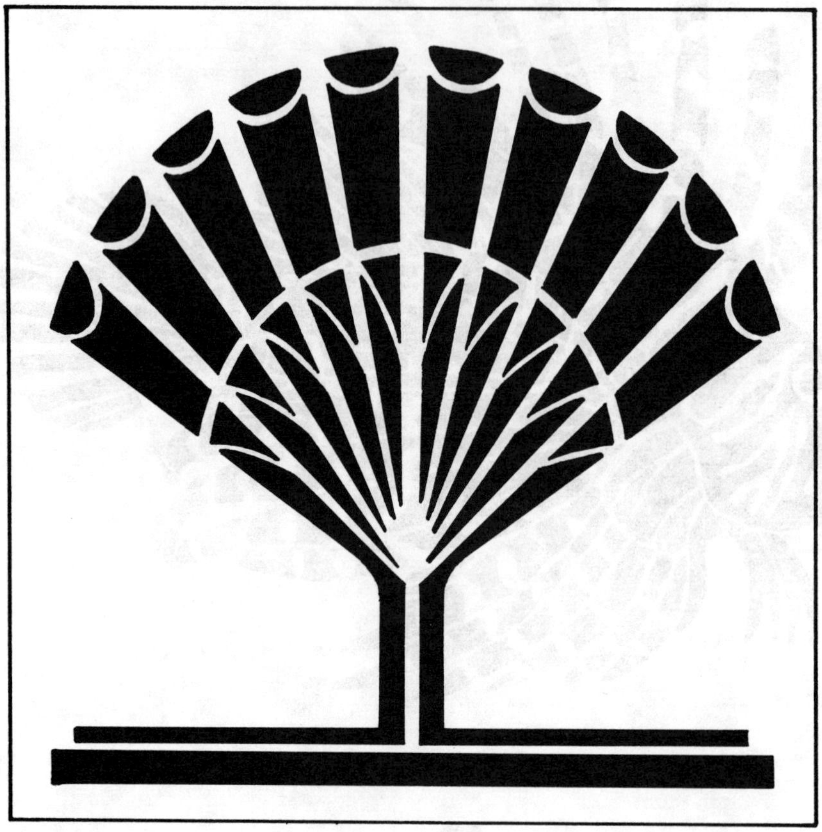

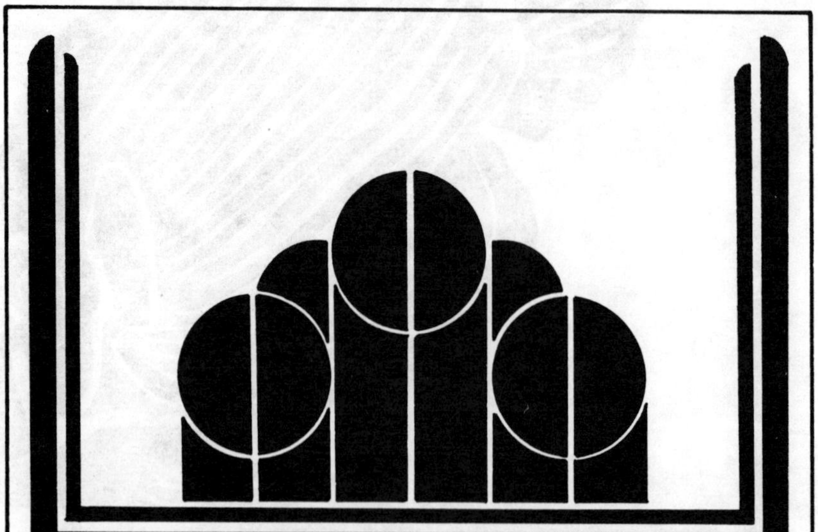

38

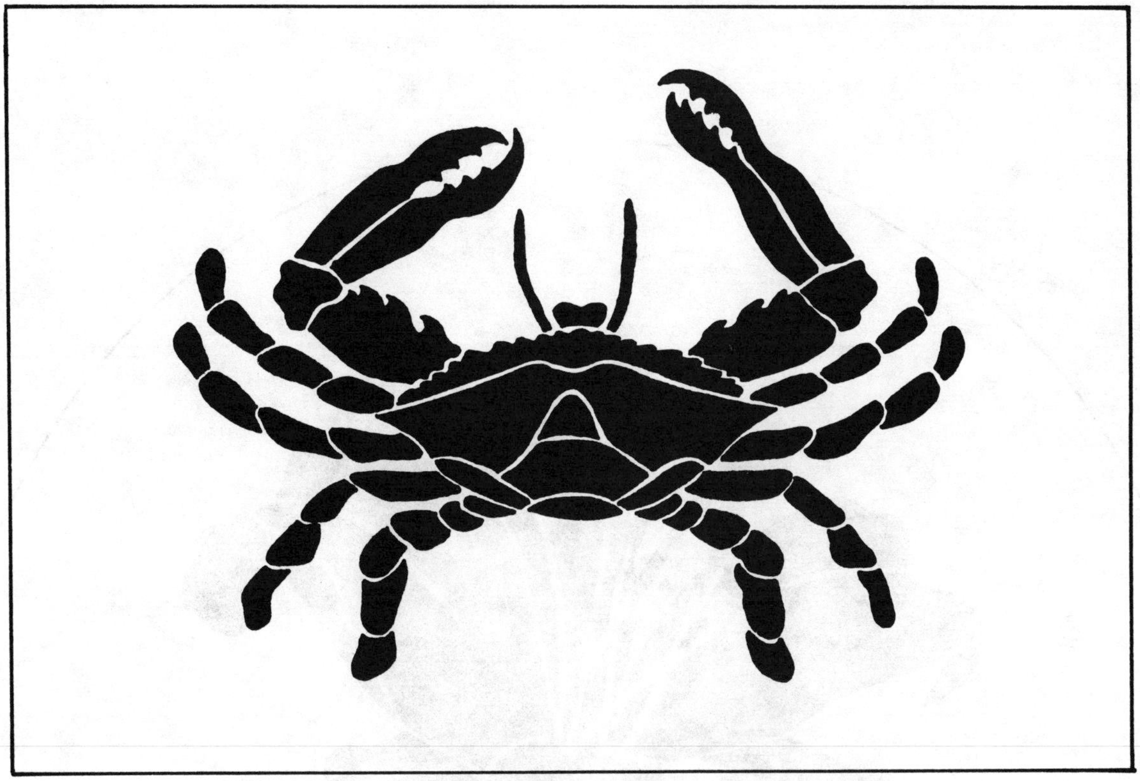

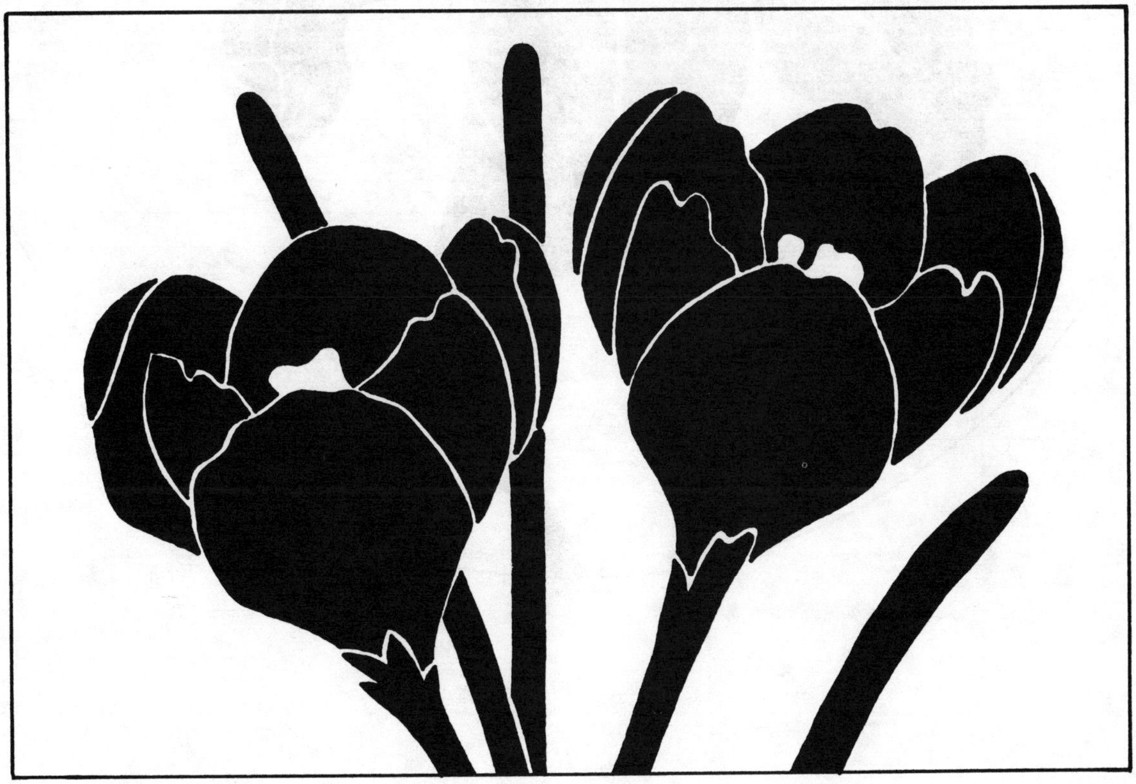

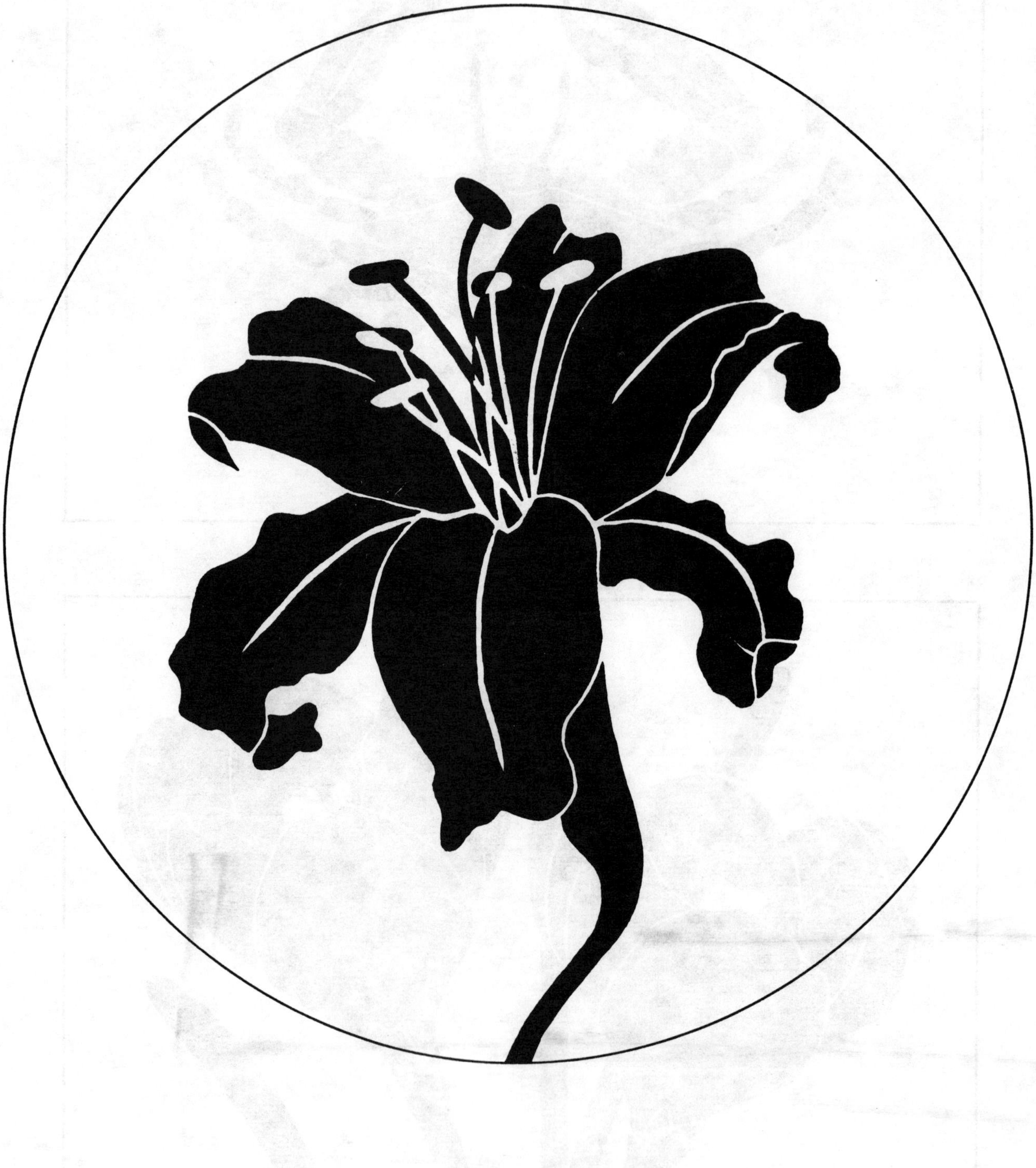

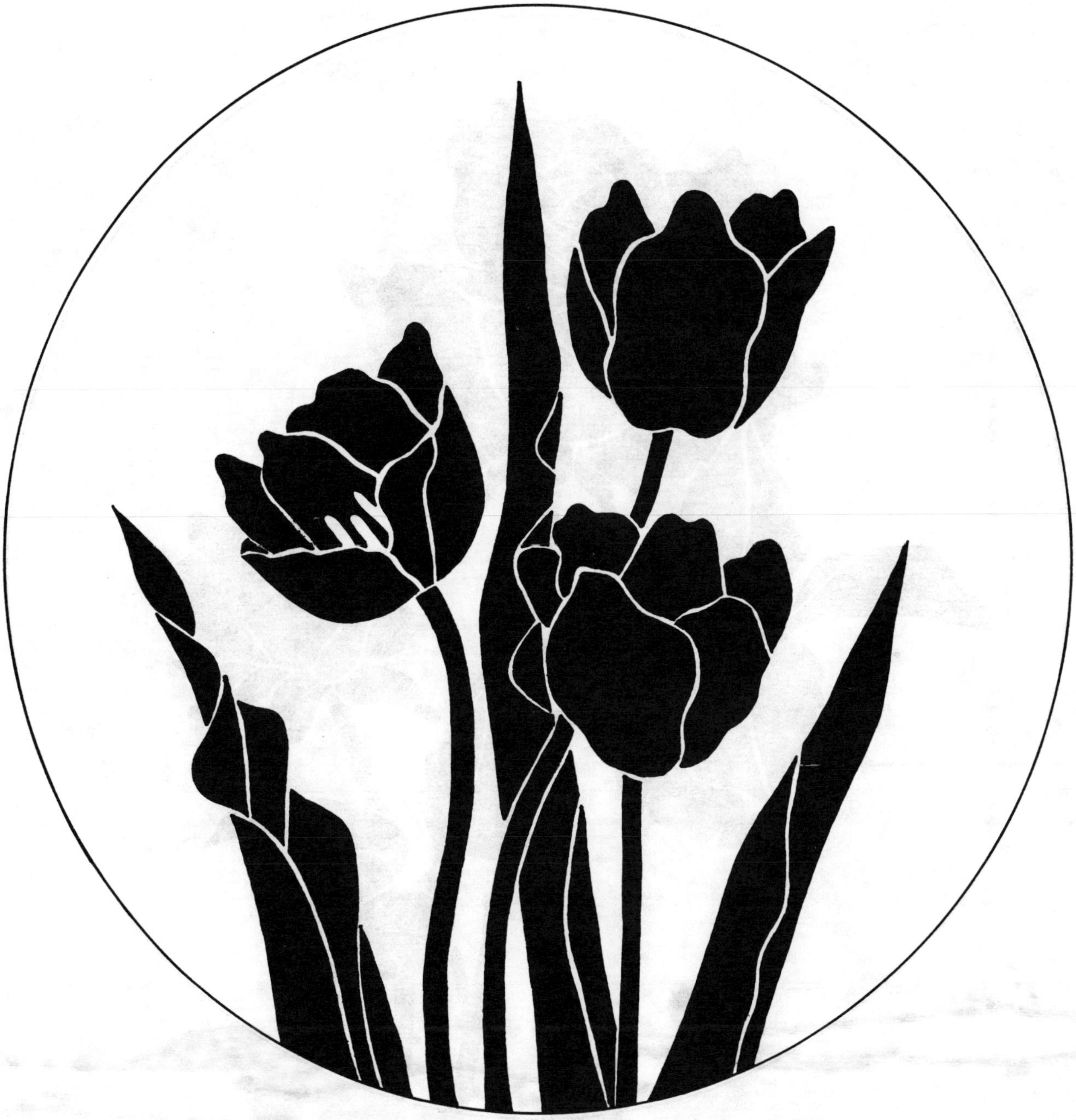

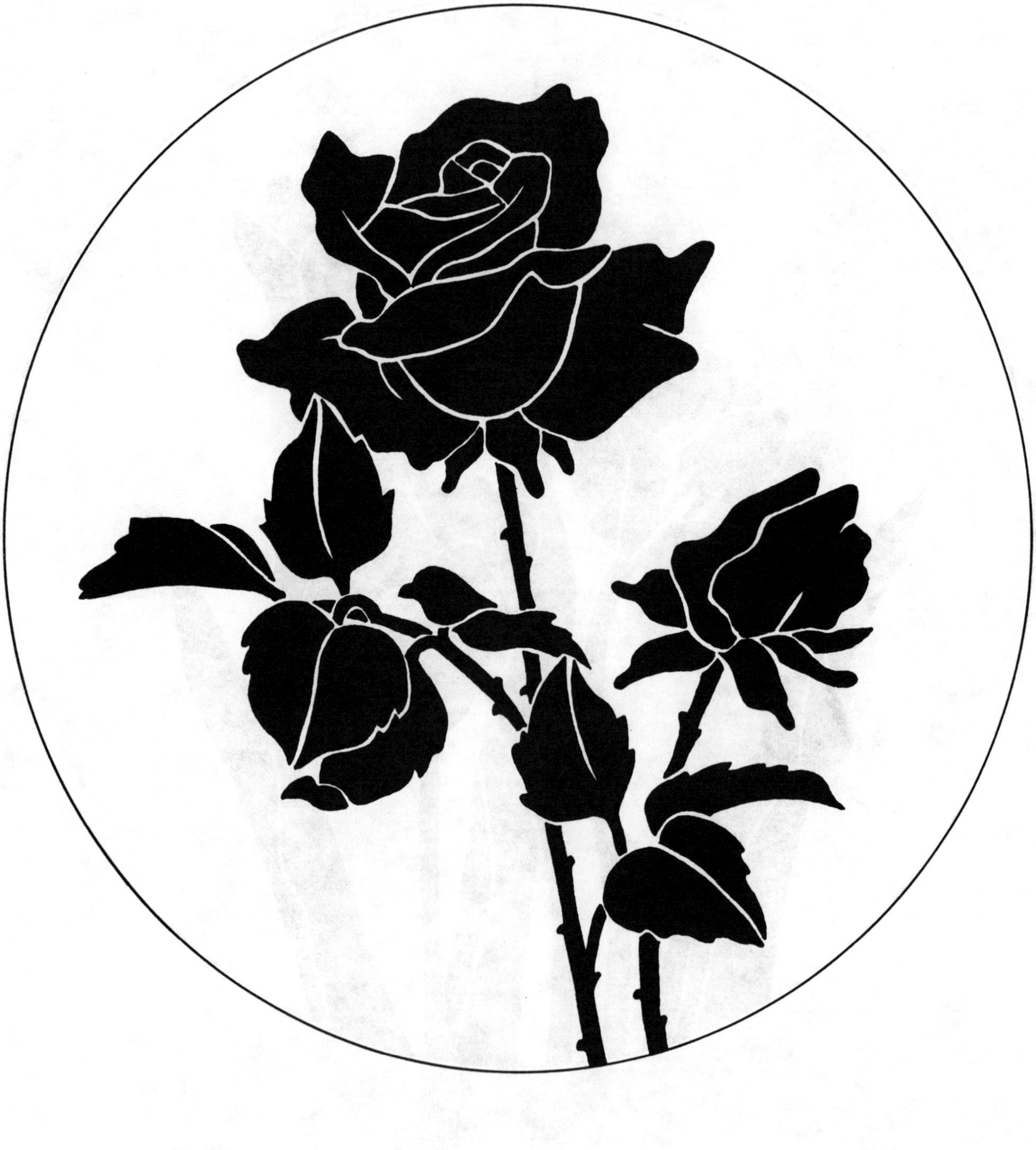

43

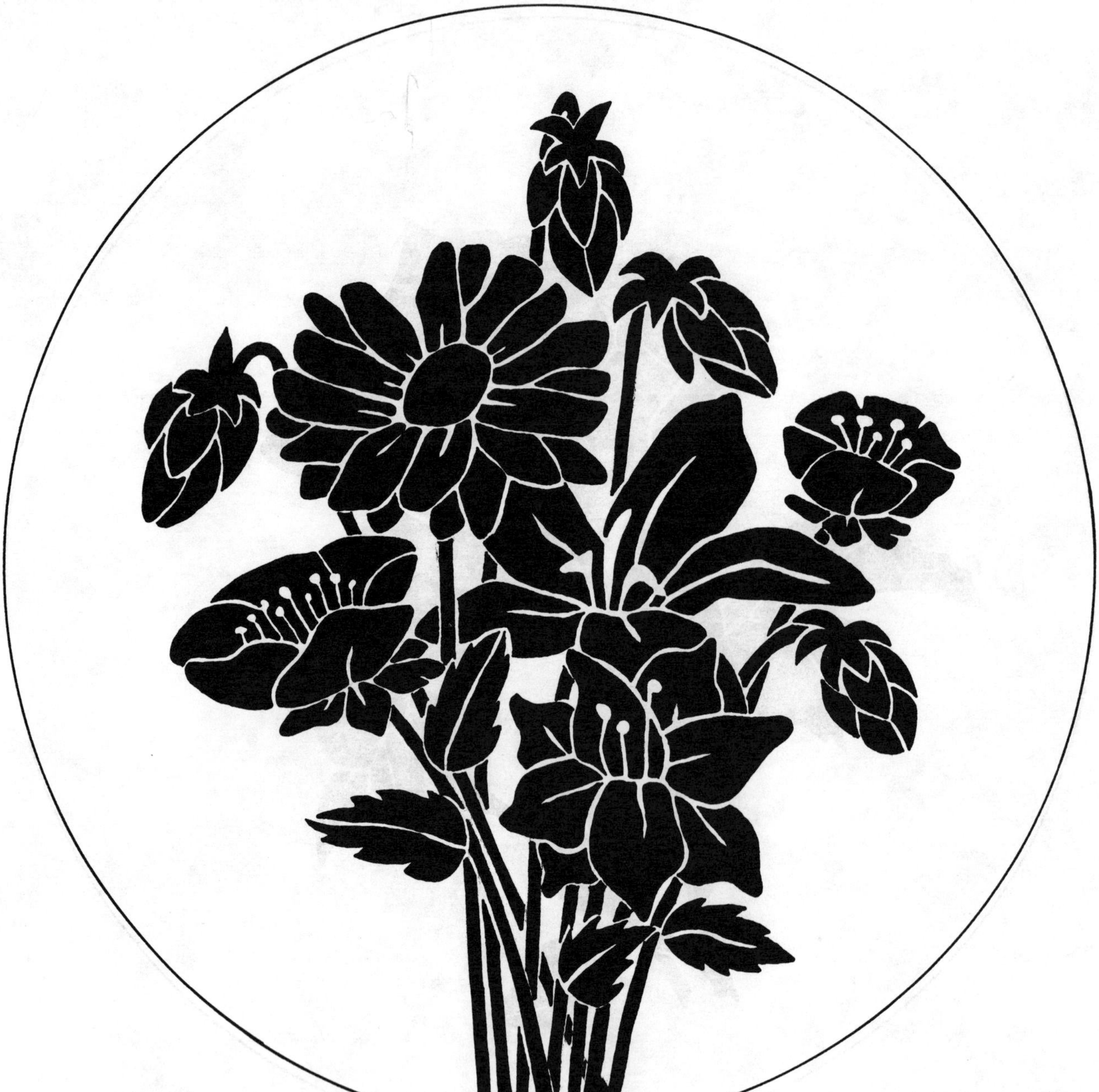

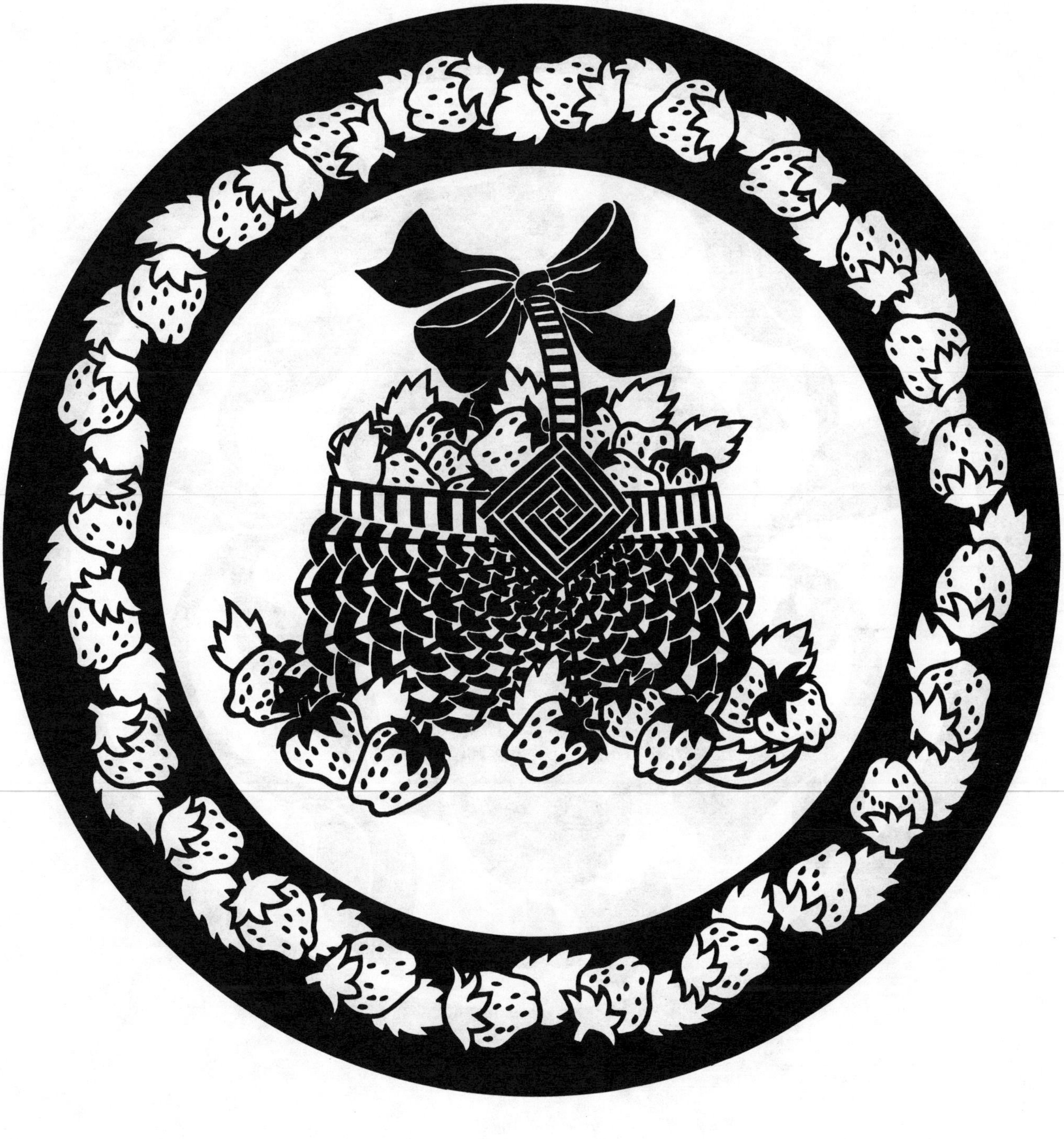

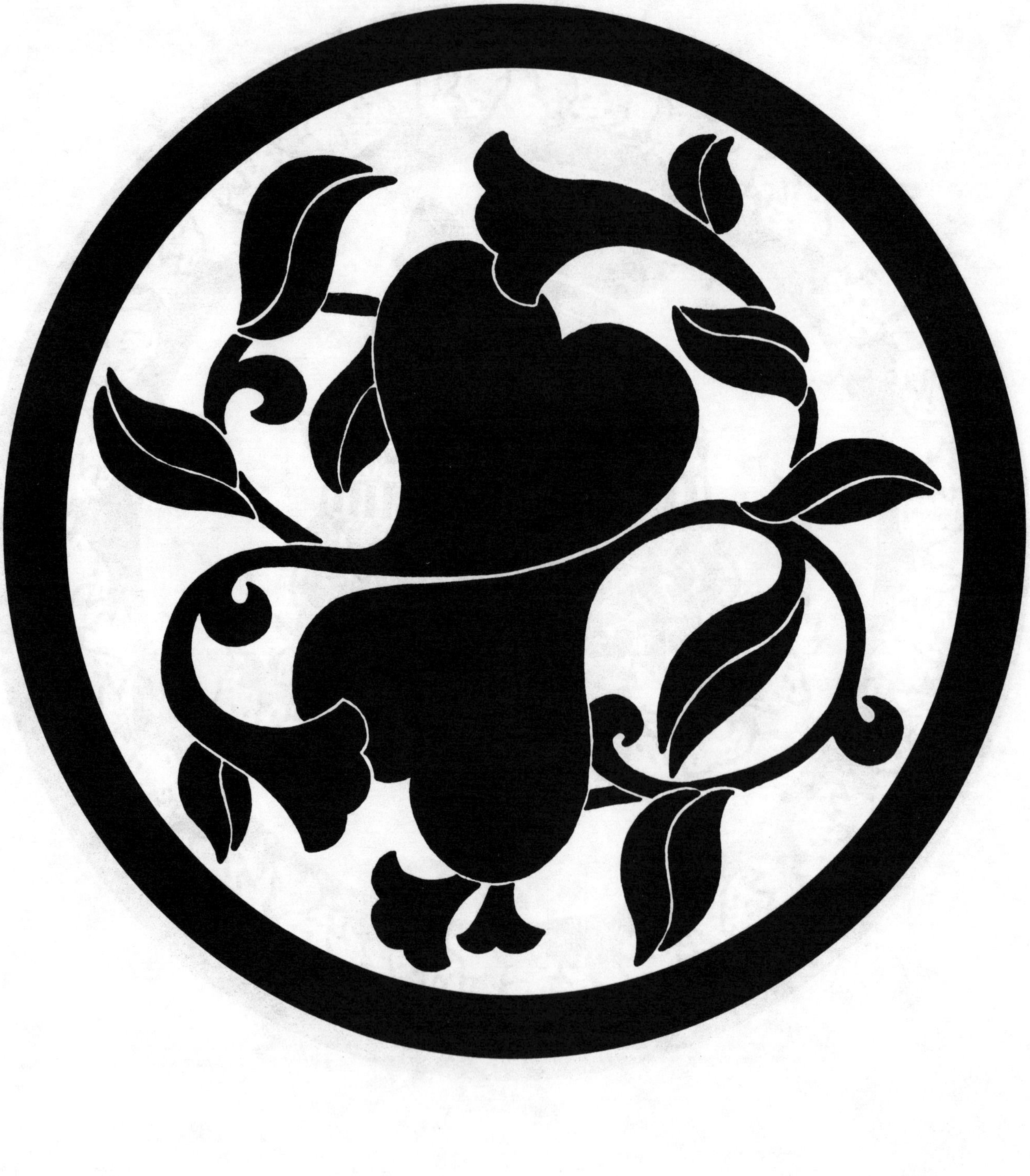

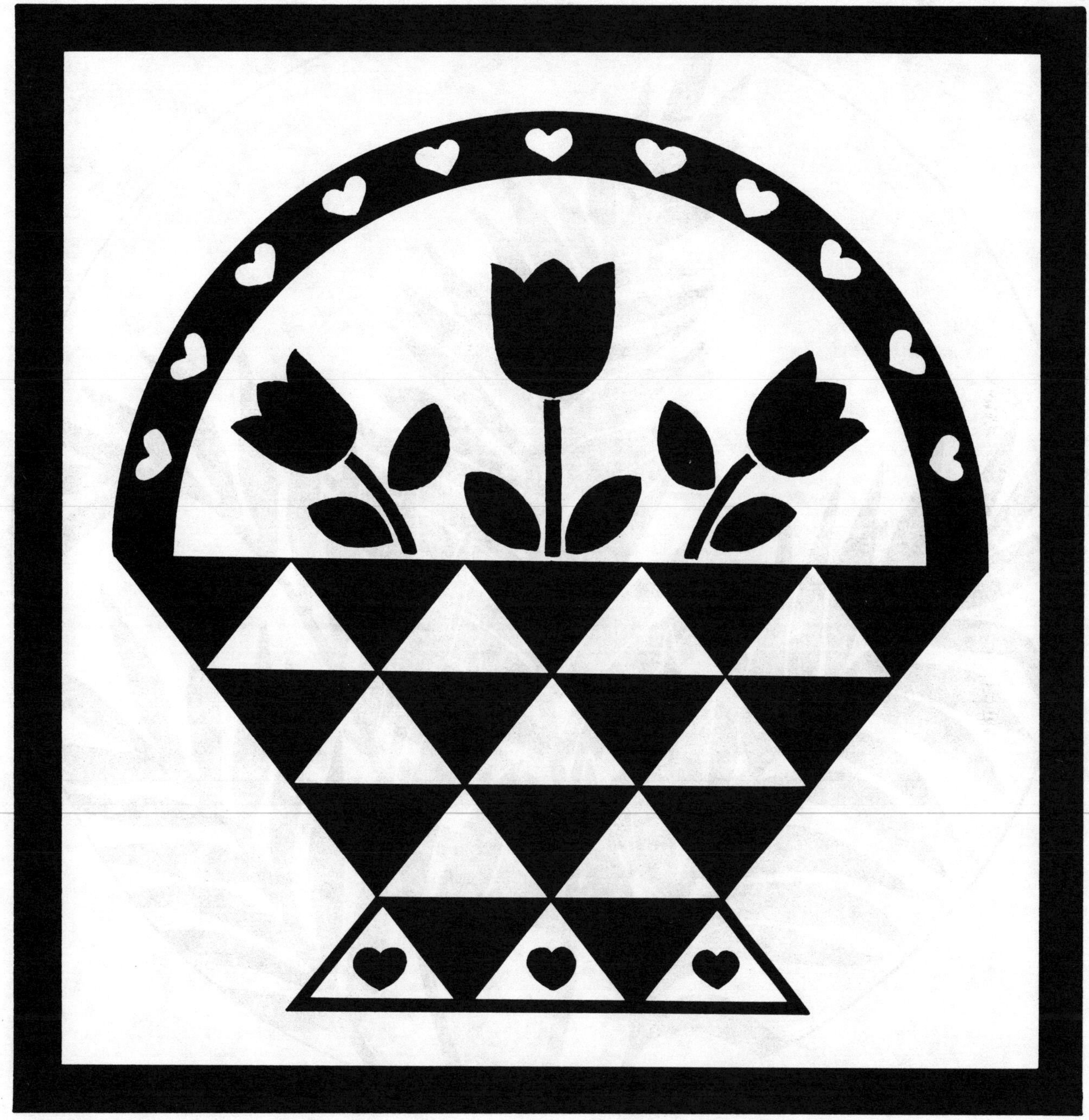

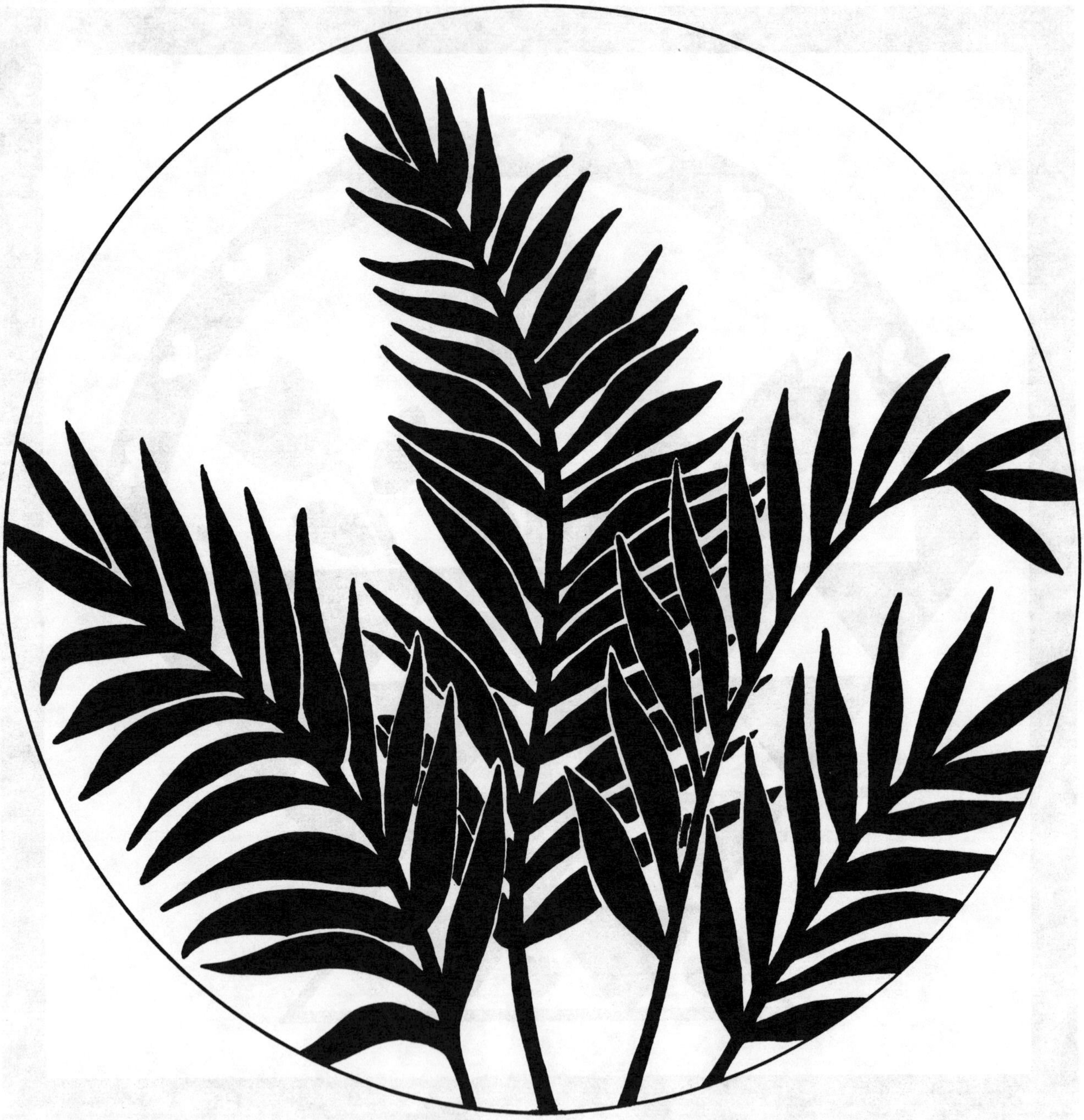

49

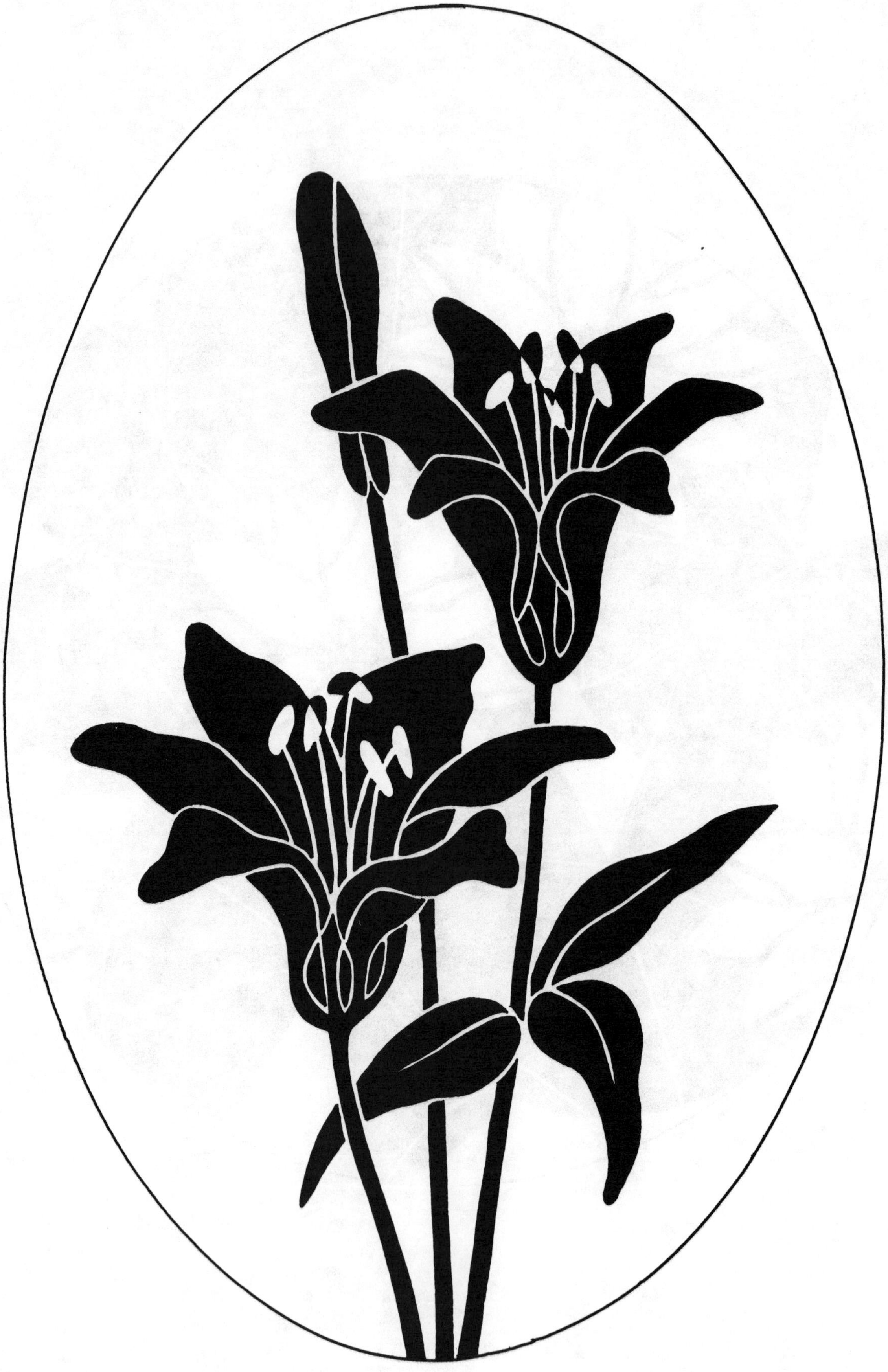

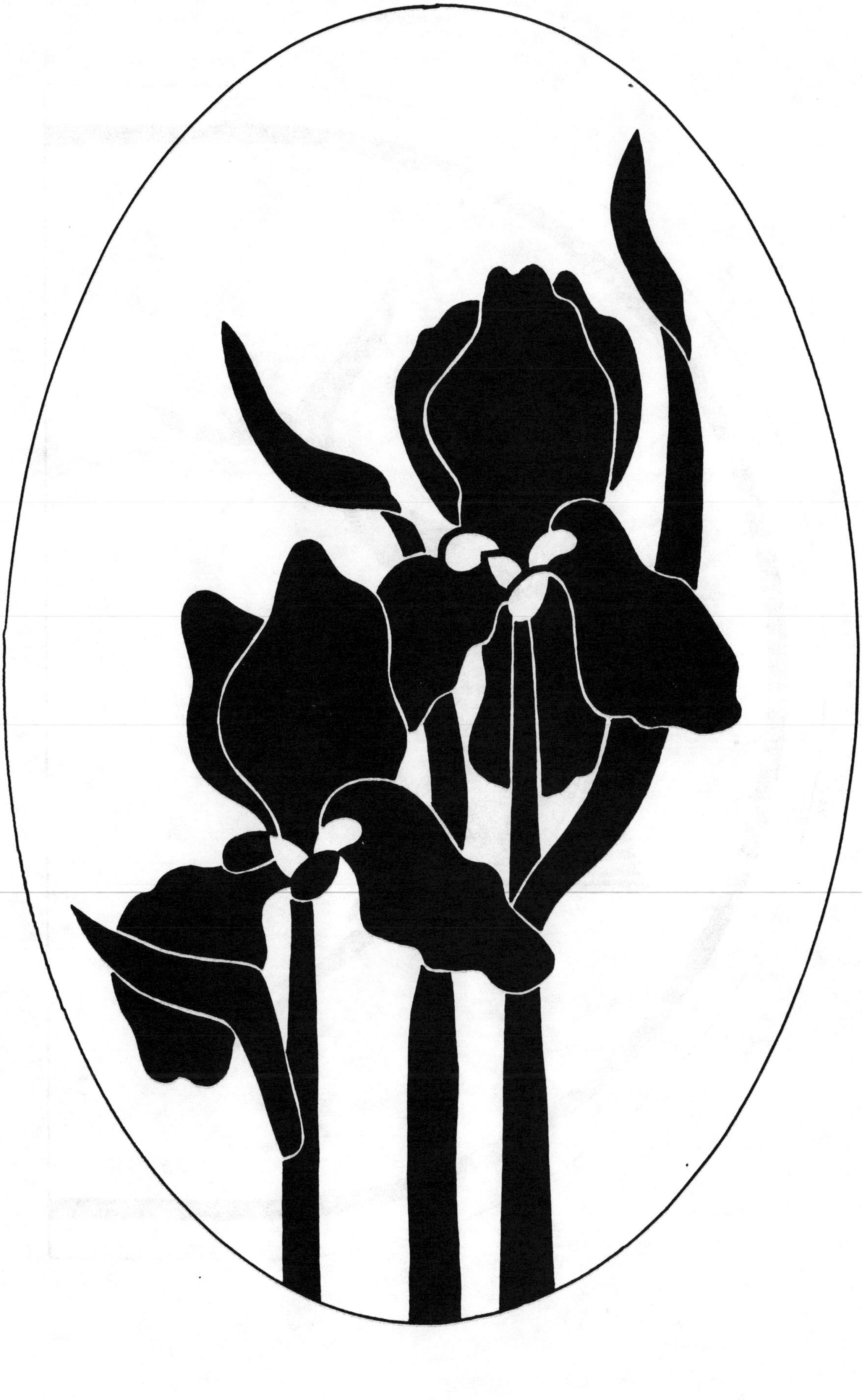

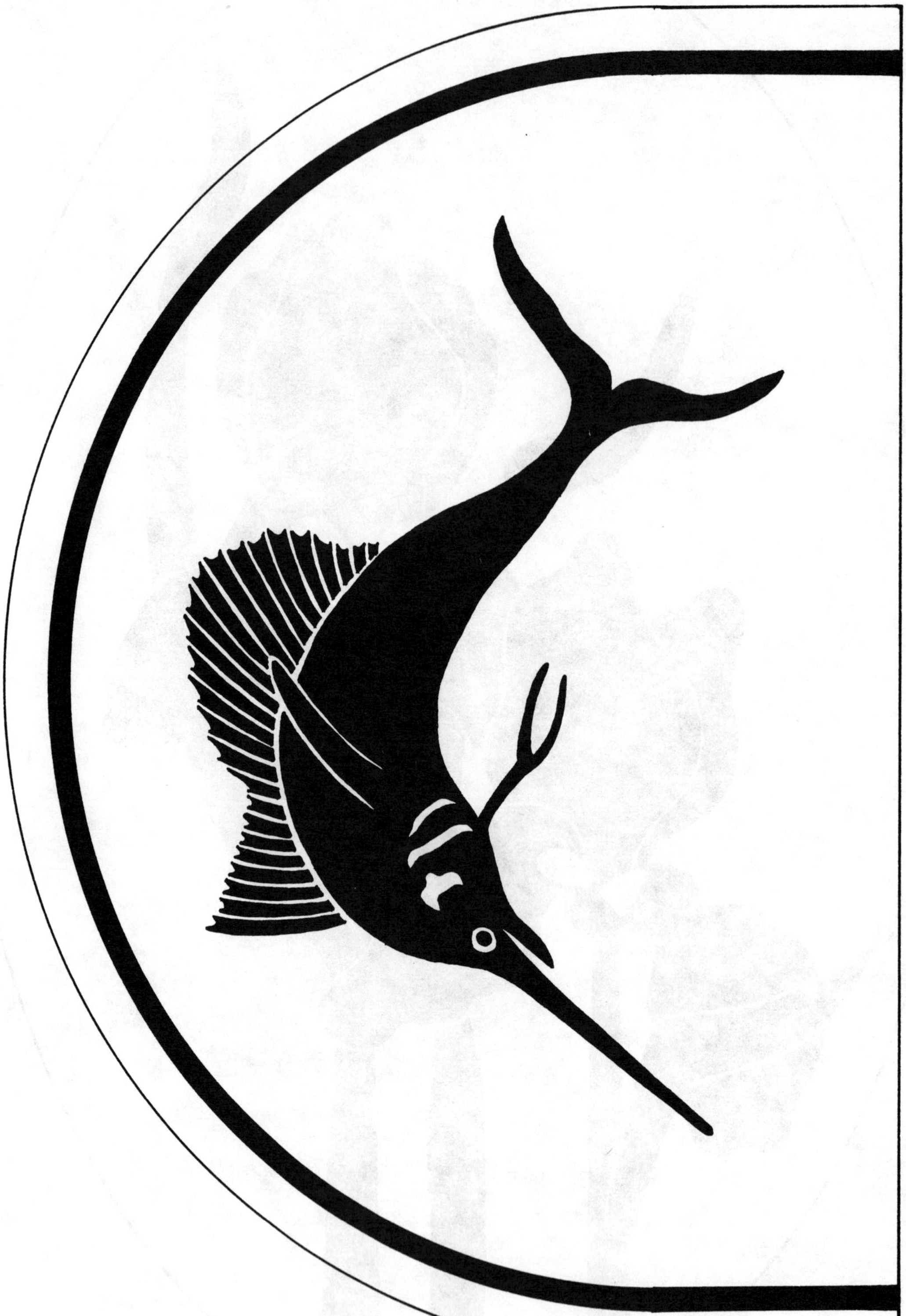

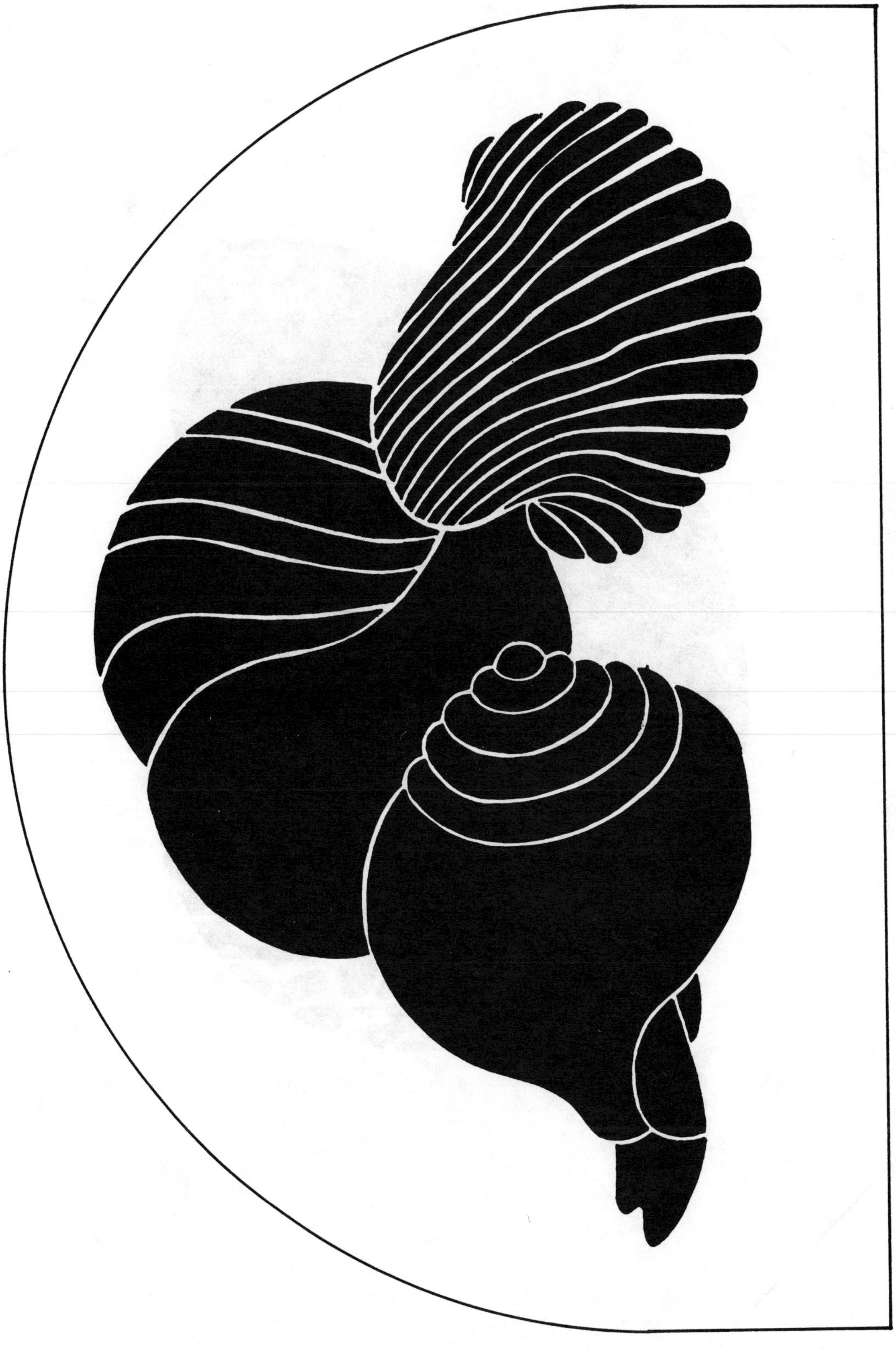

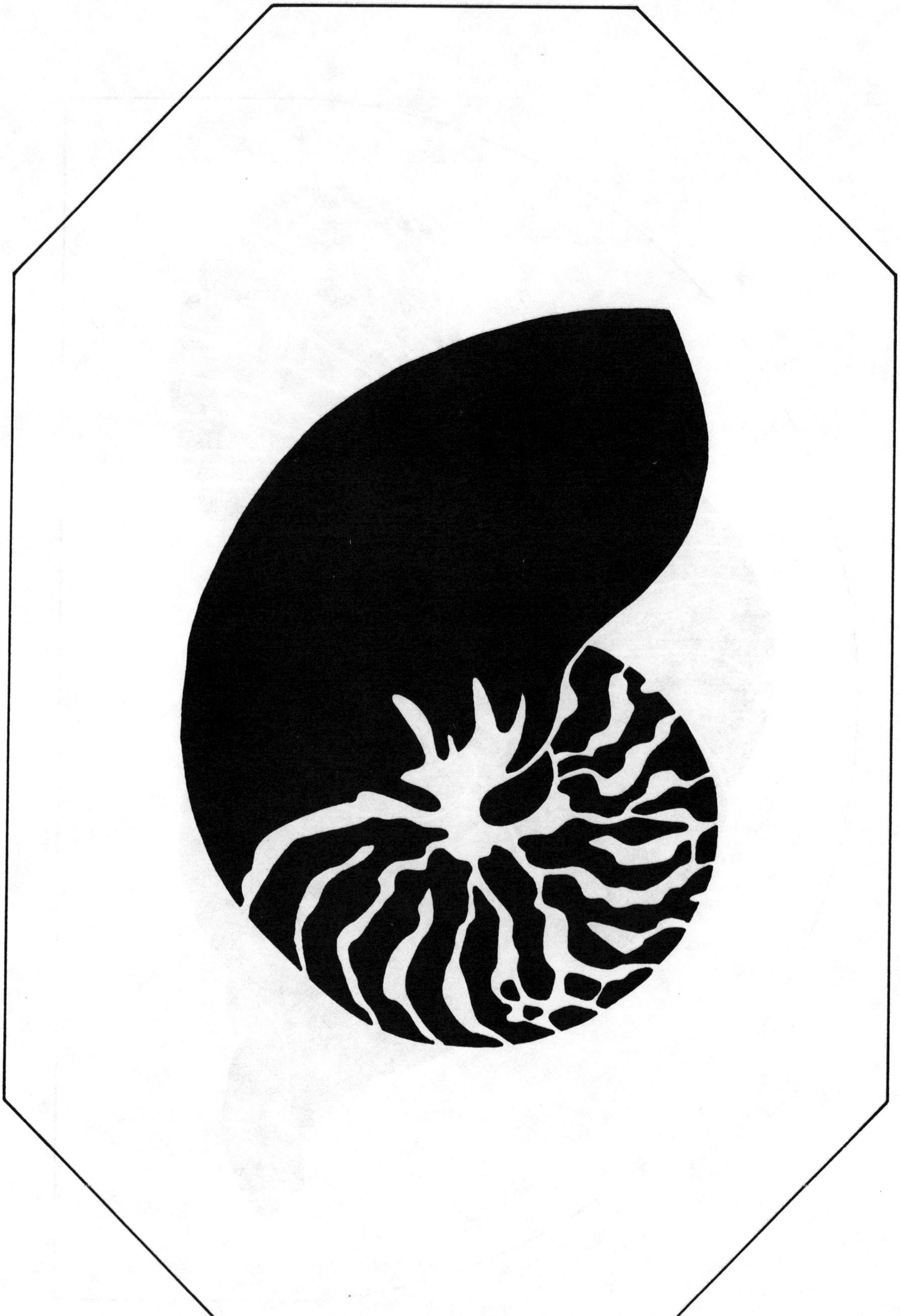

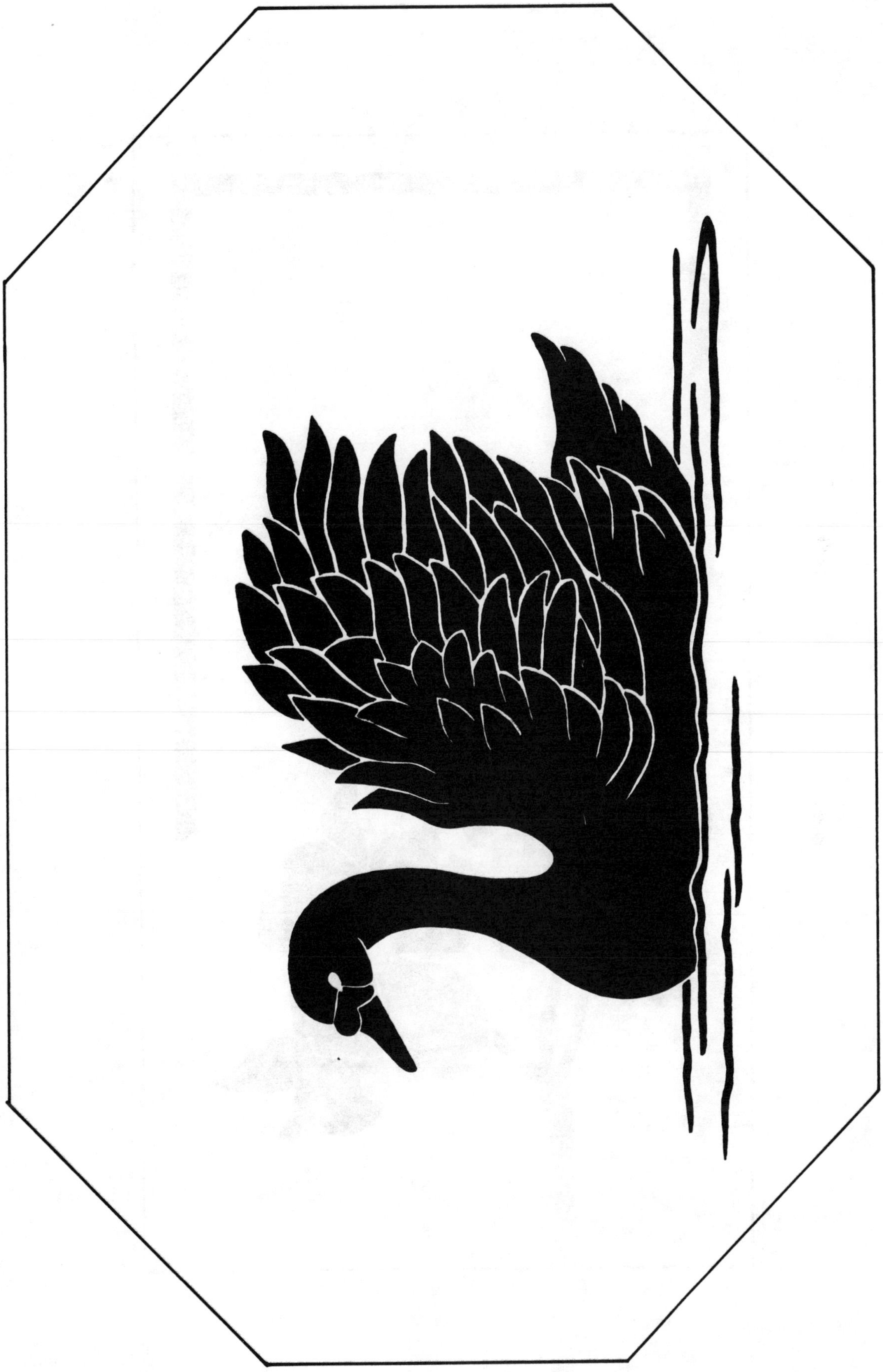

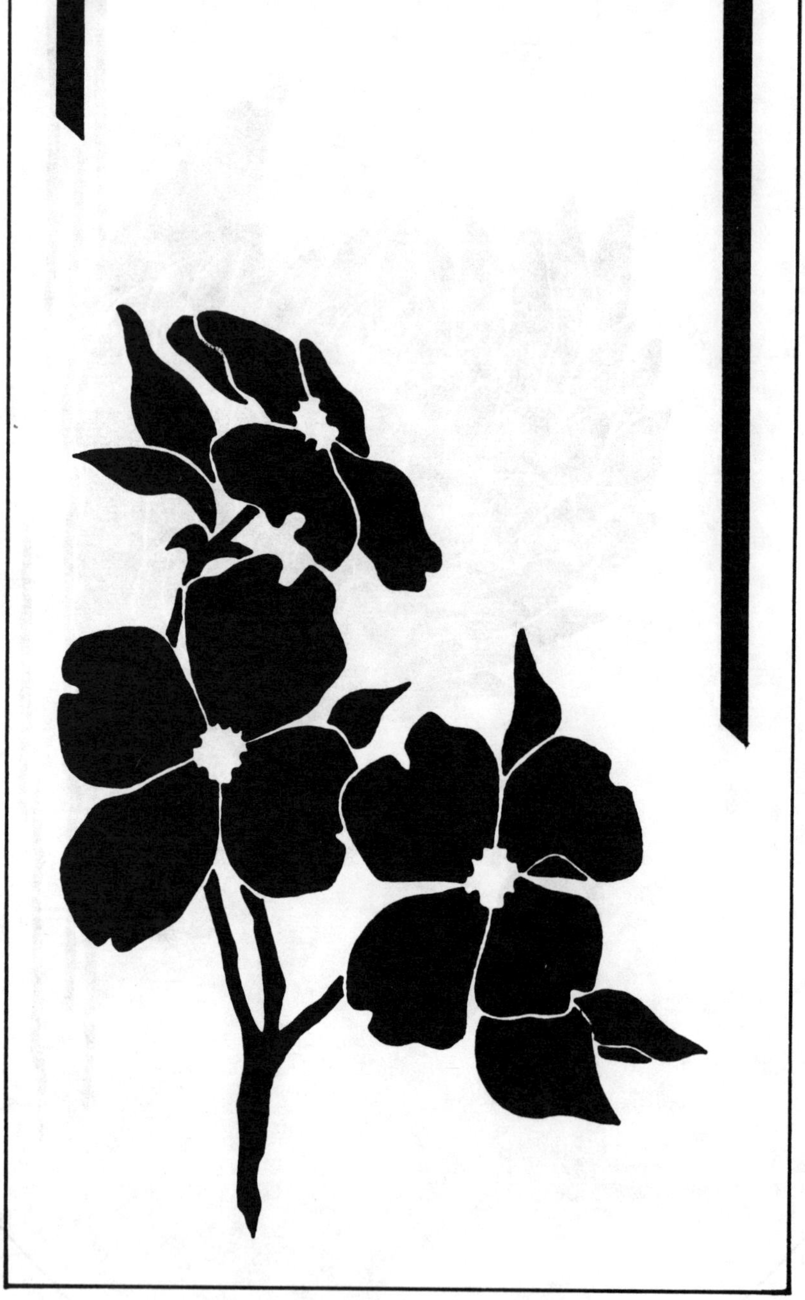

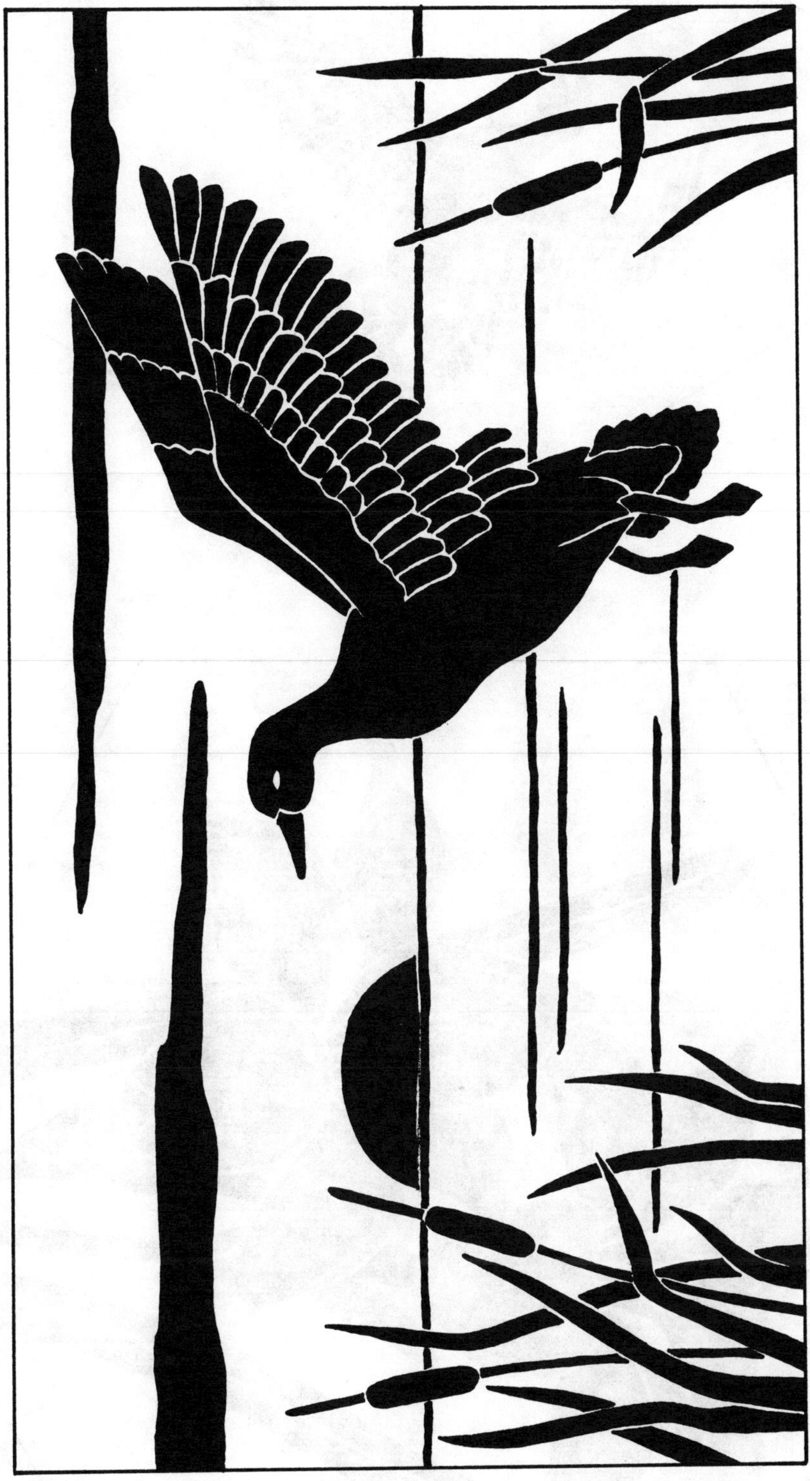

58

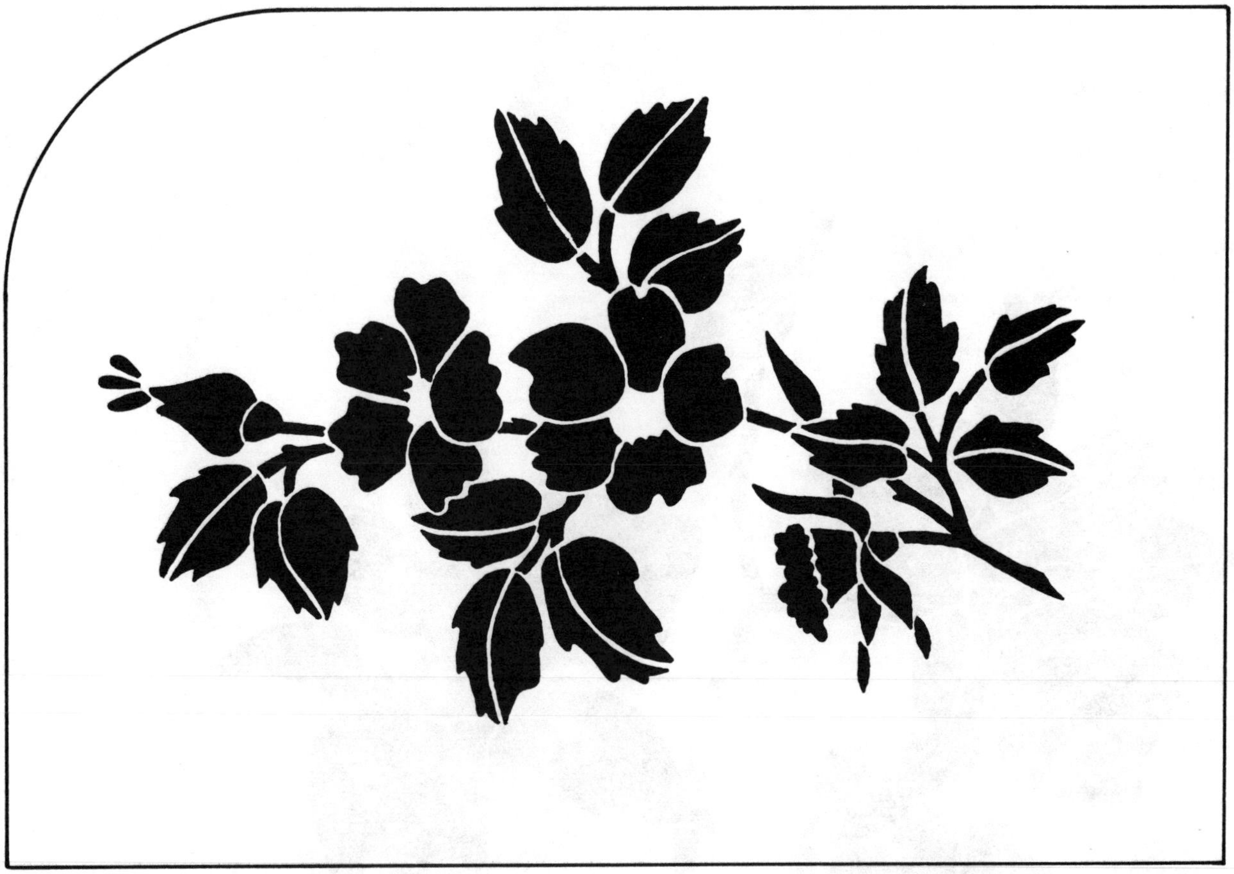

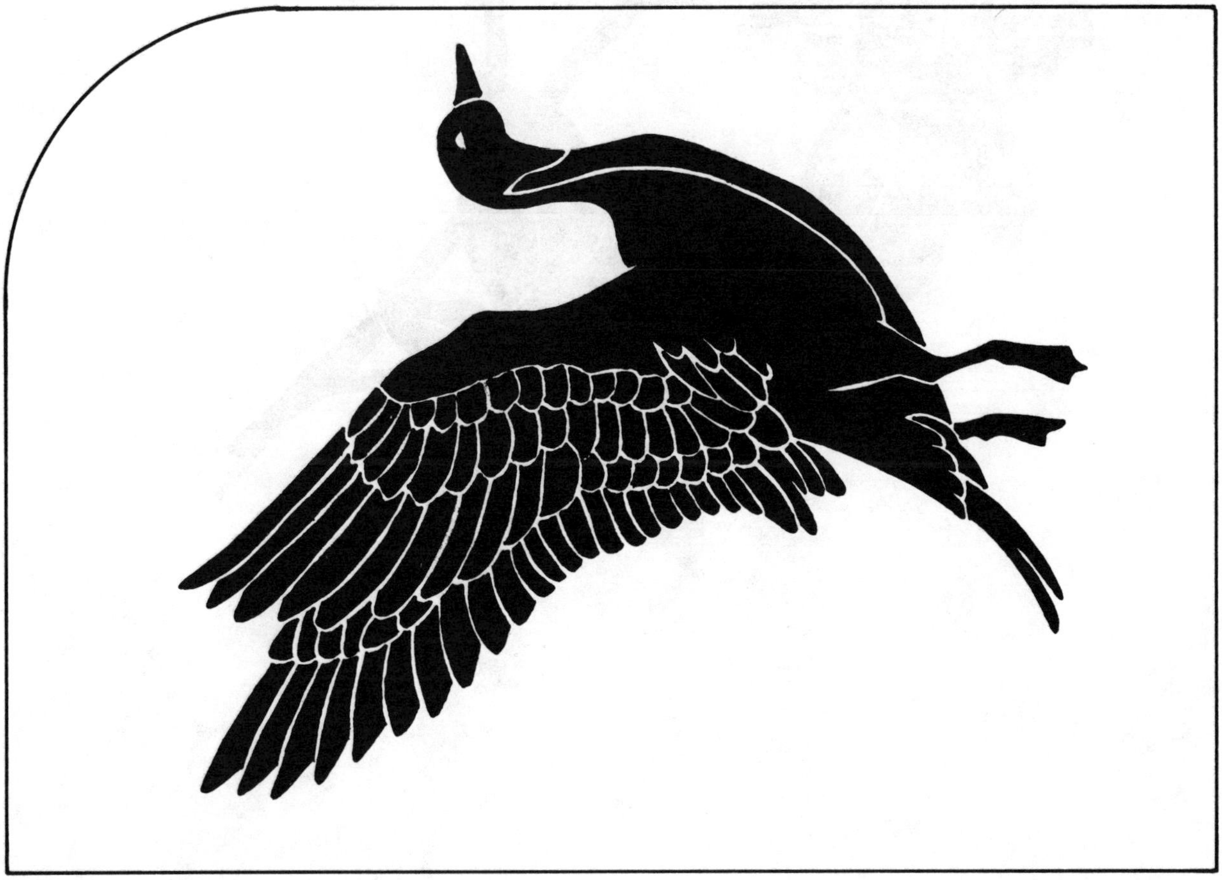

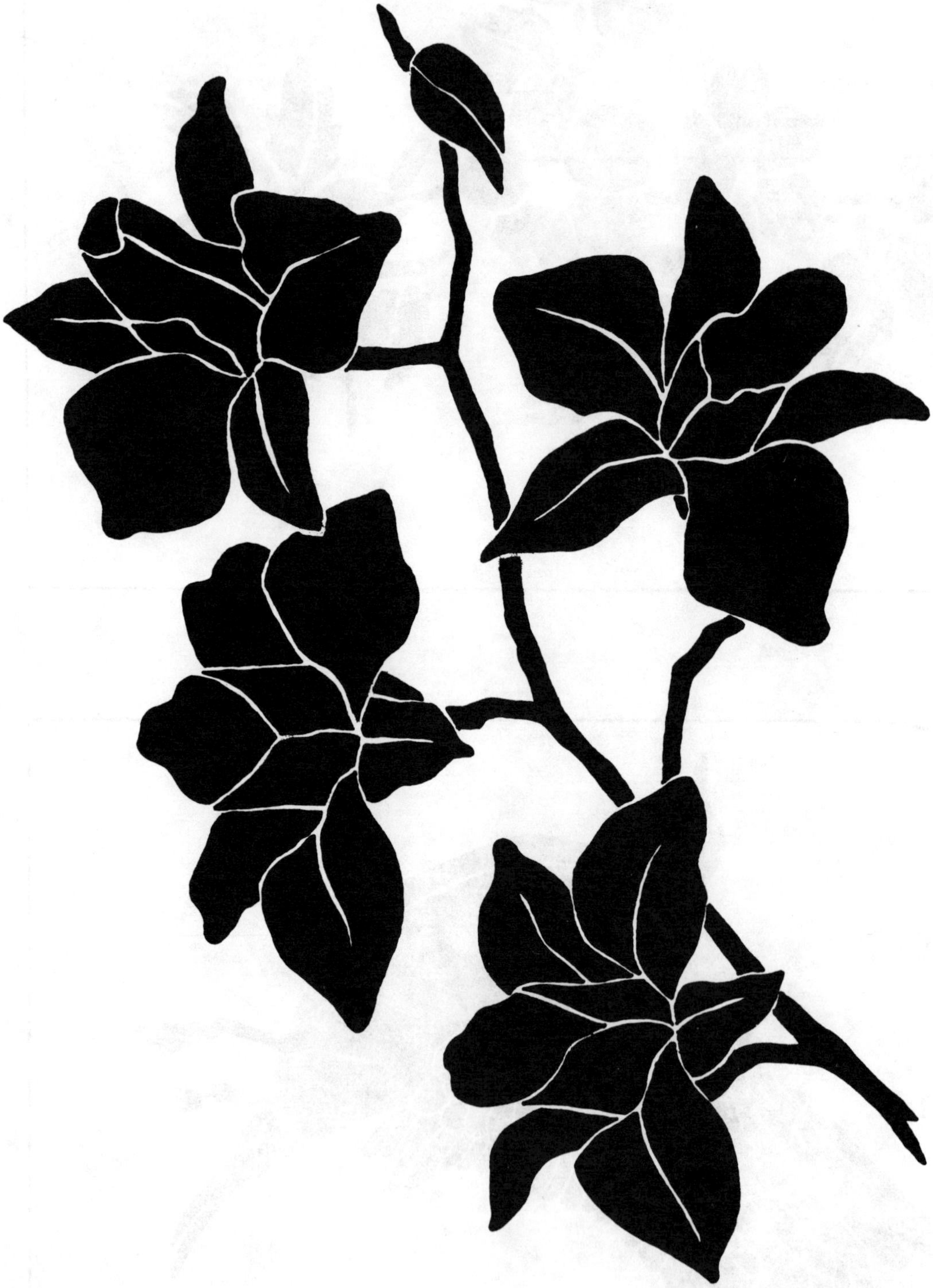

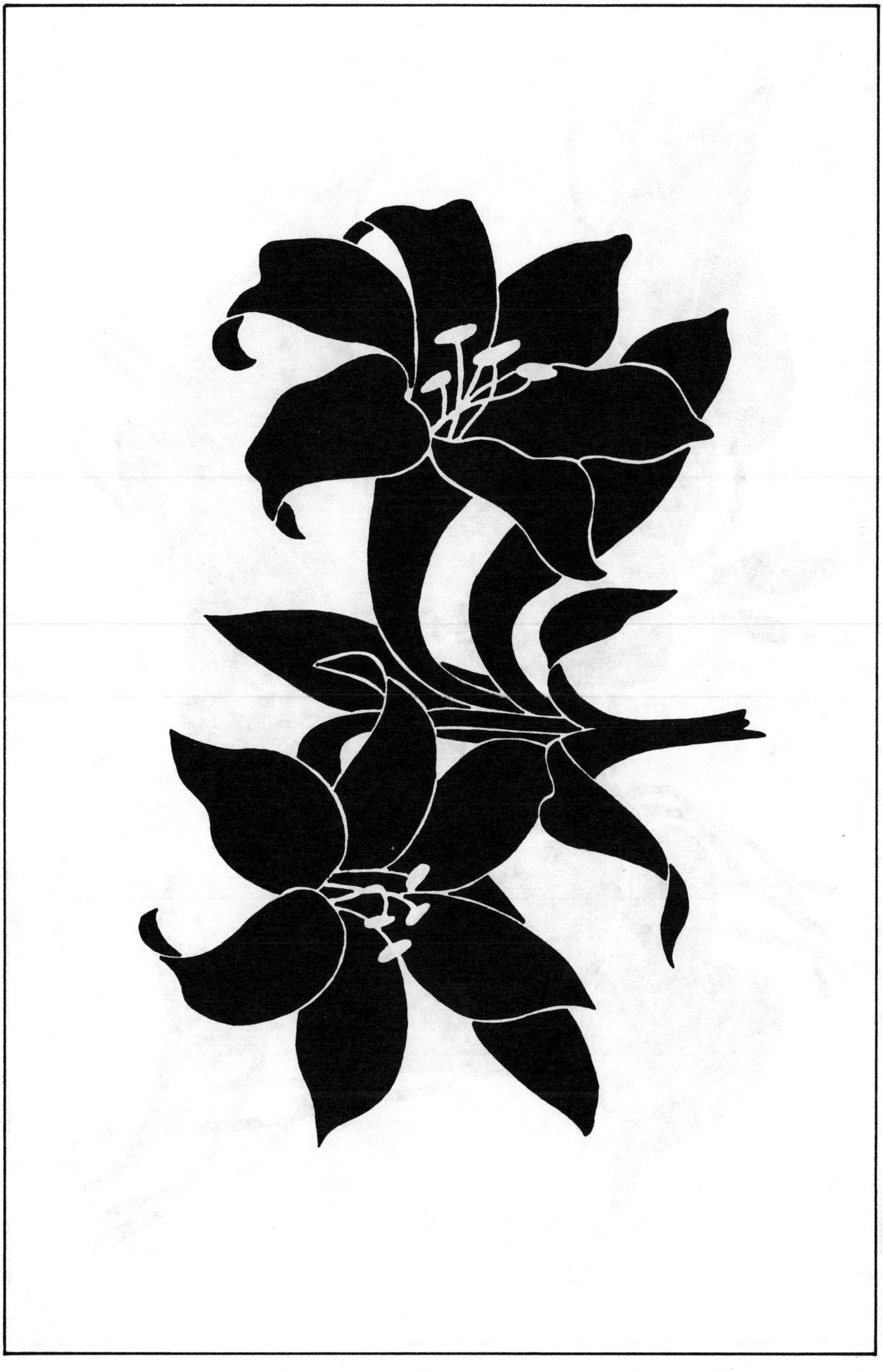

62

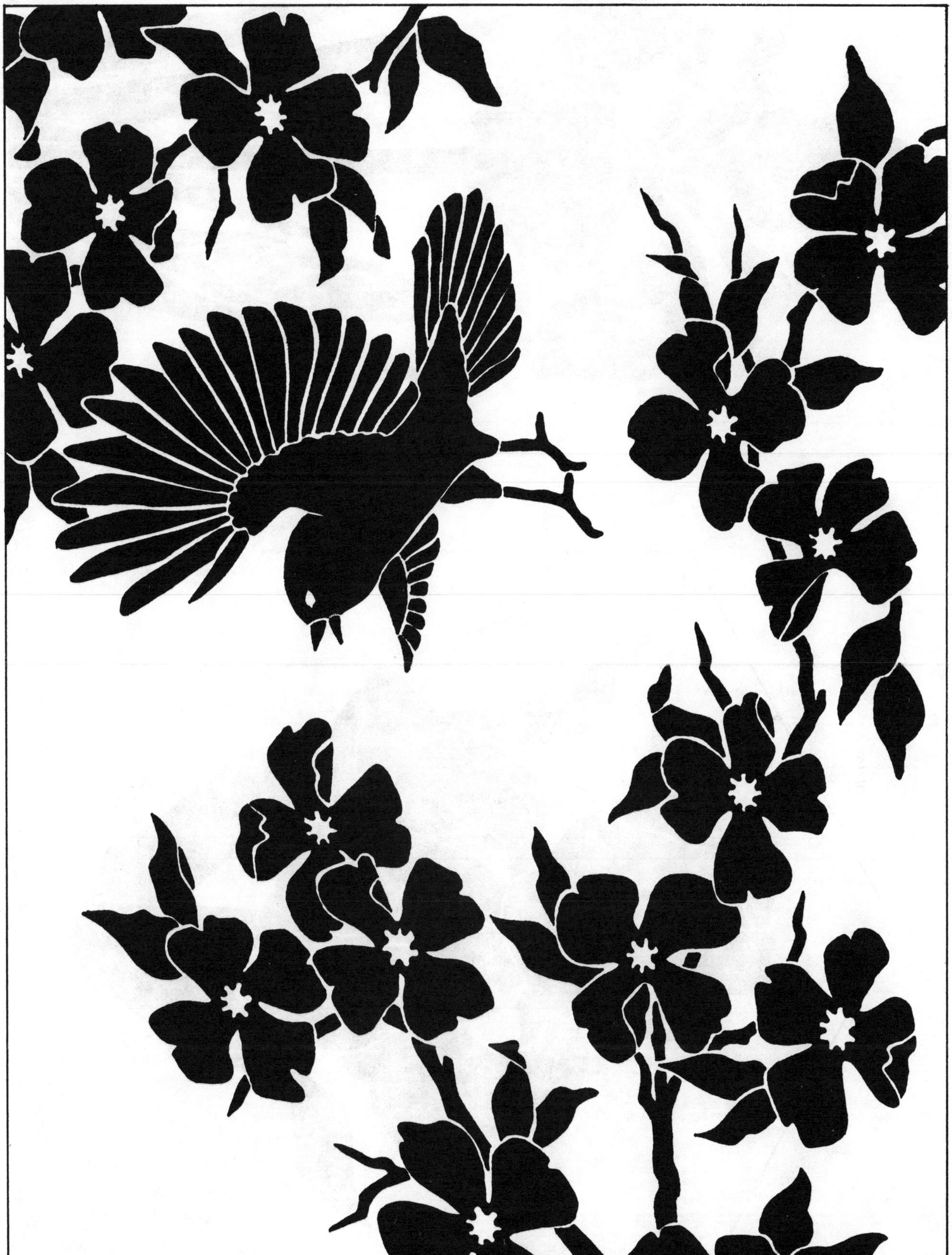

64

65

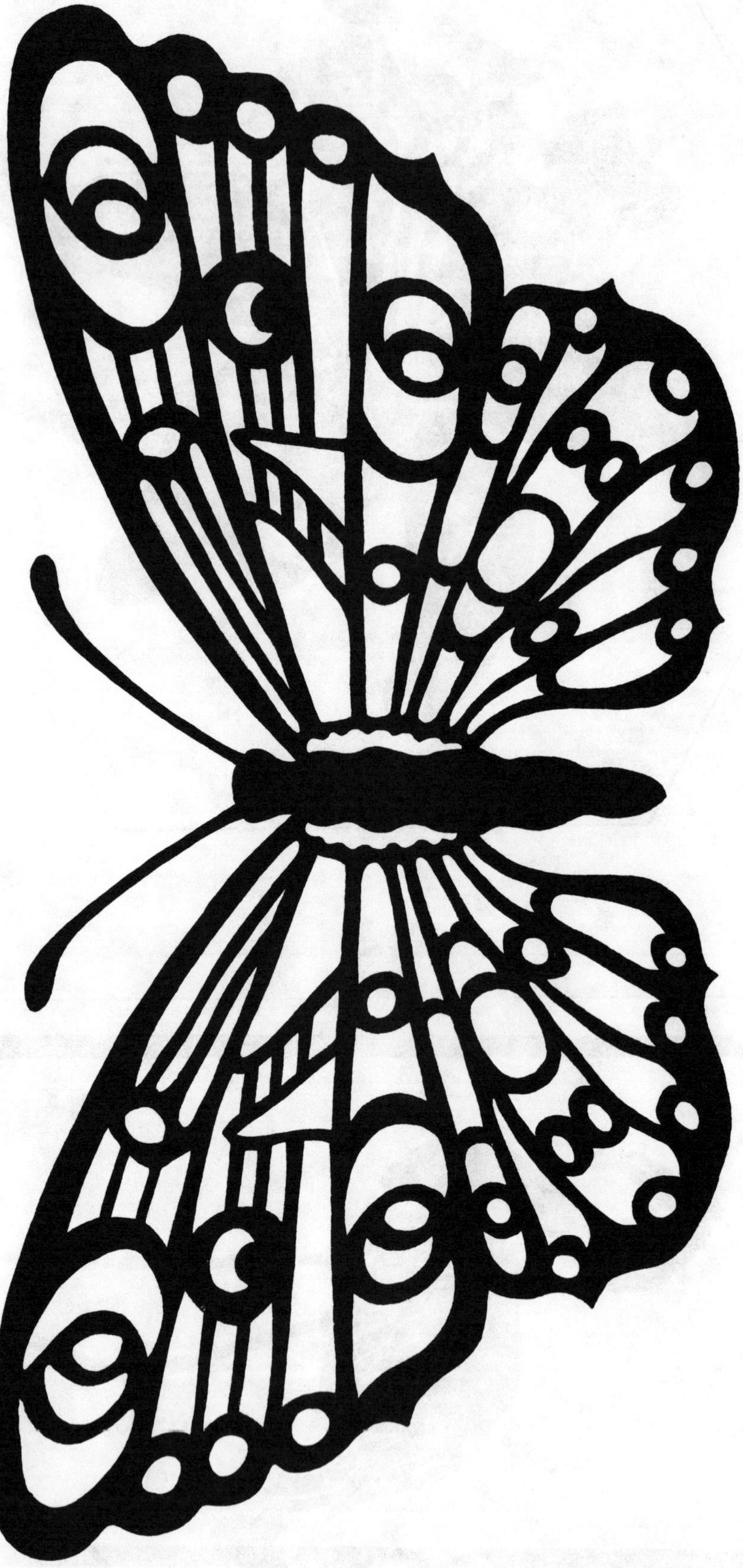

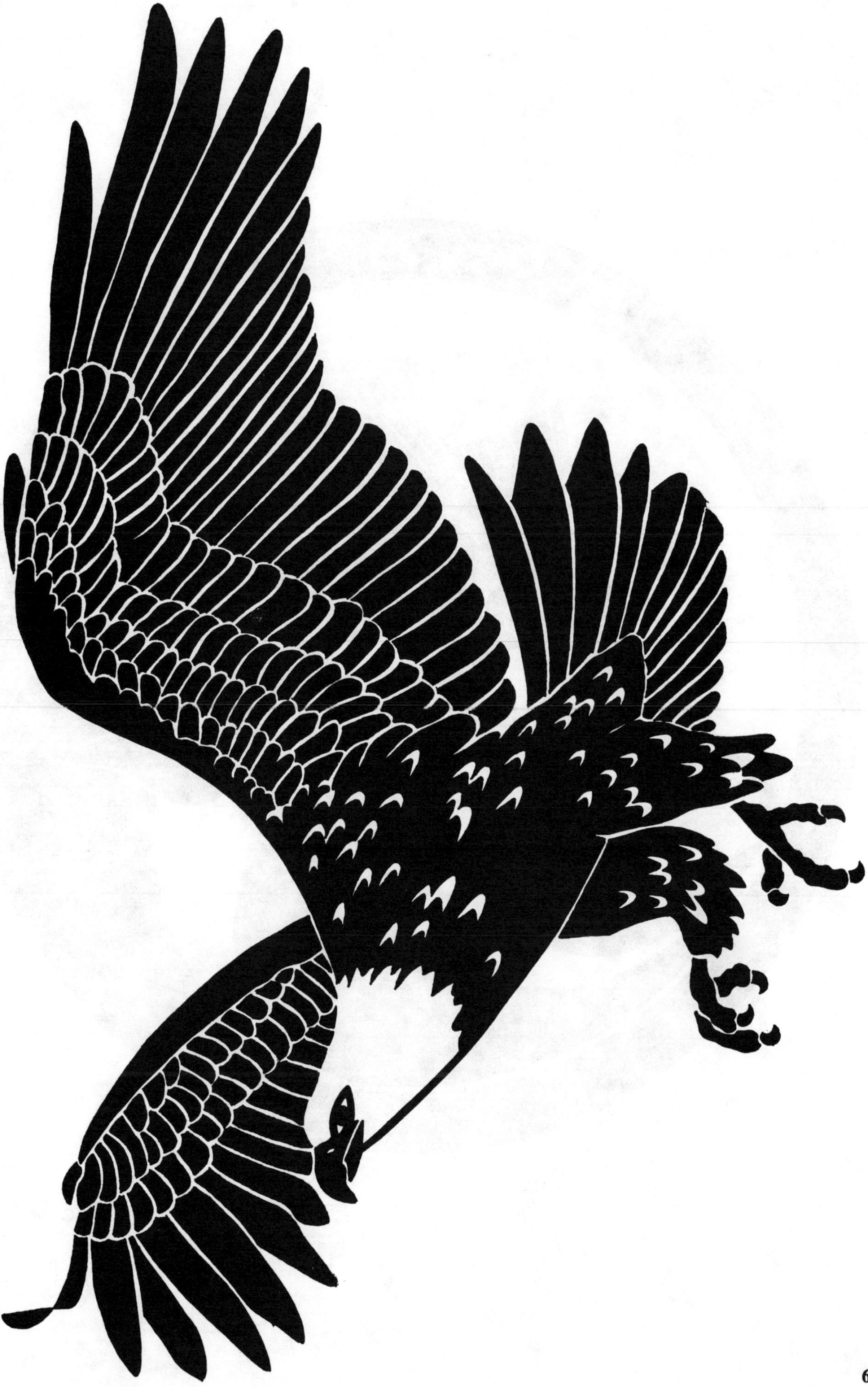

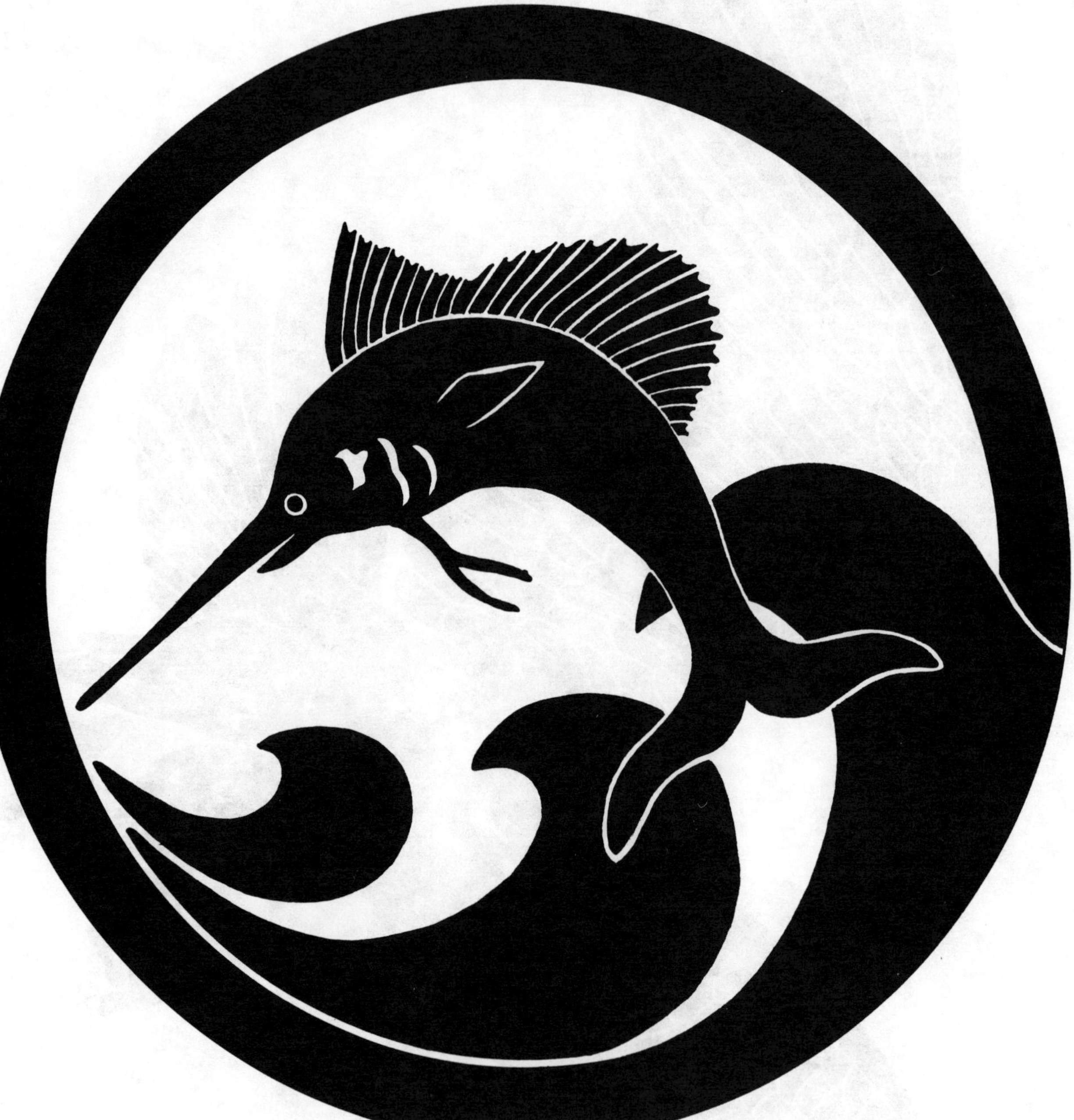

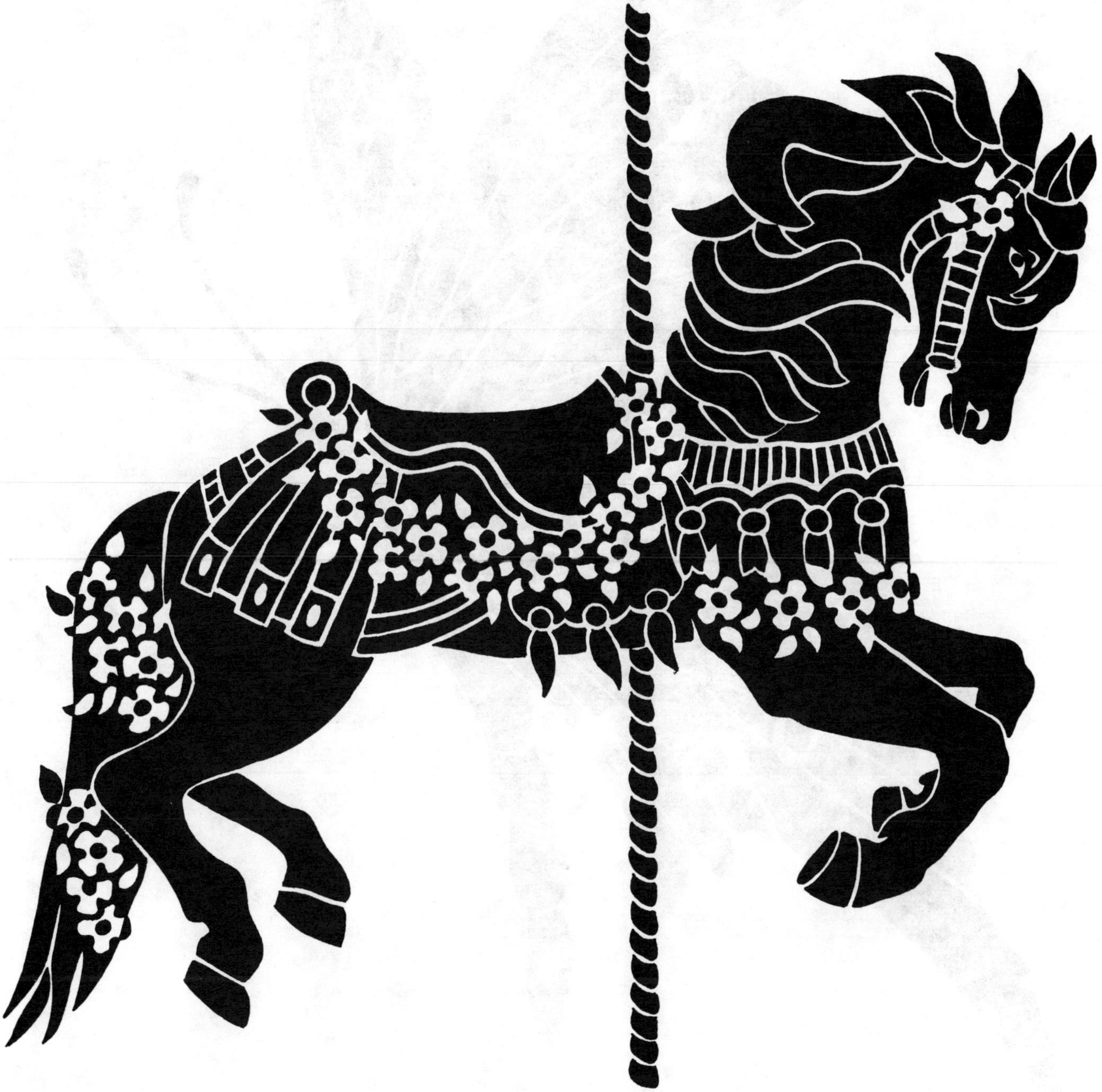

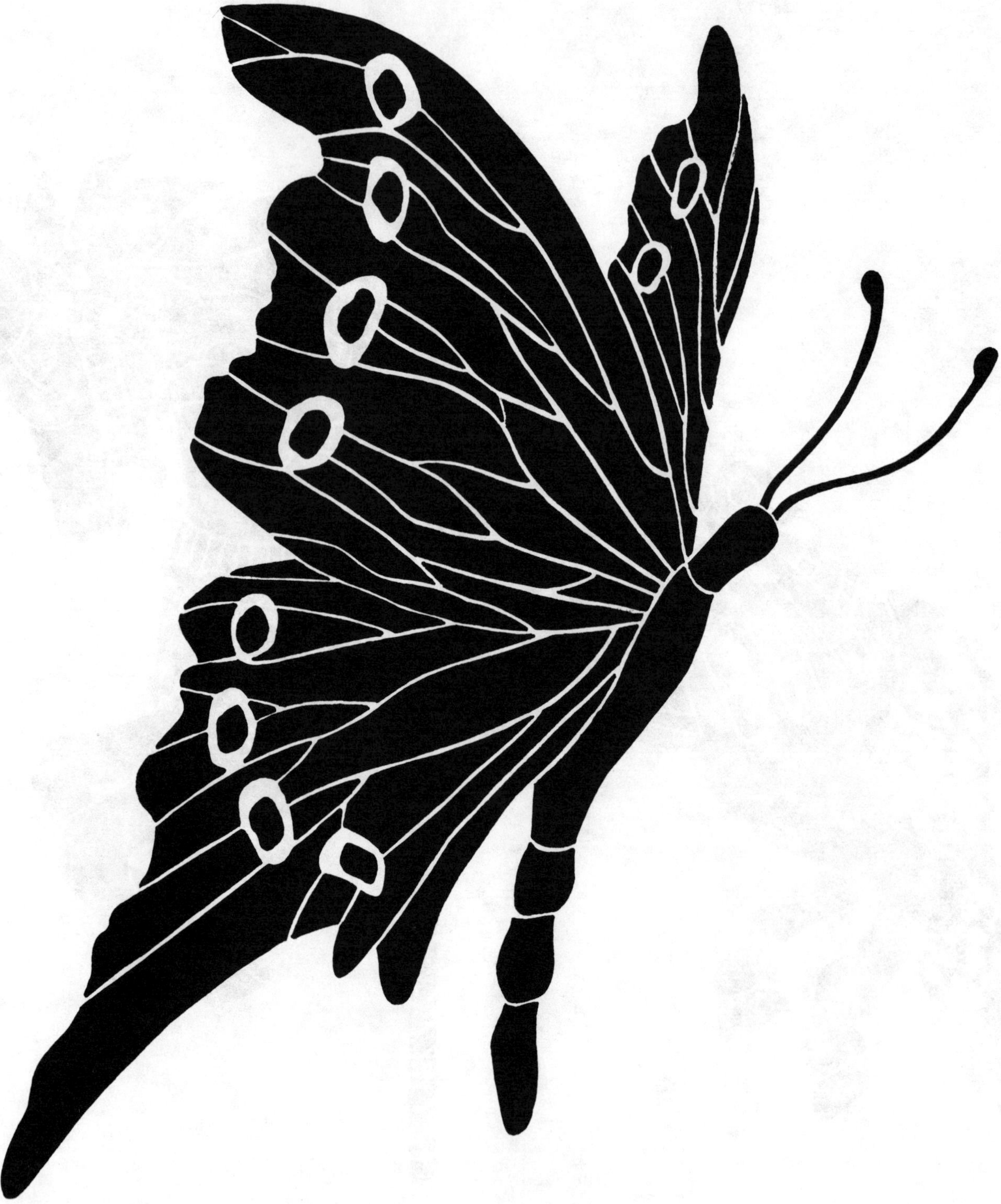

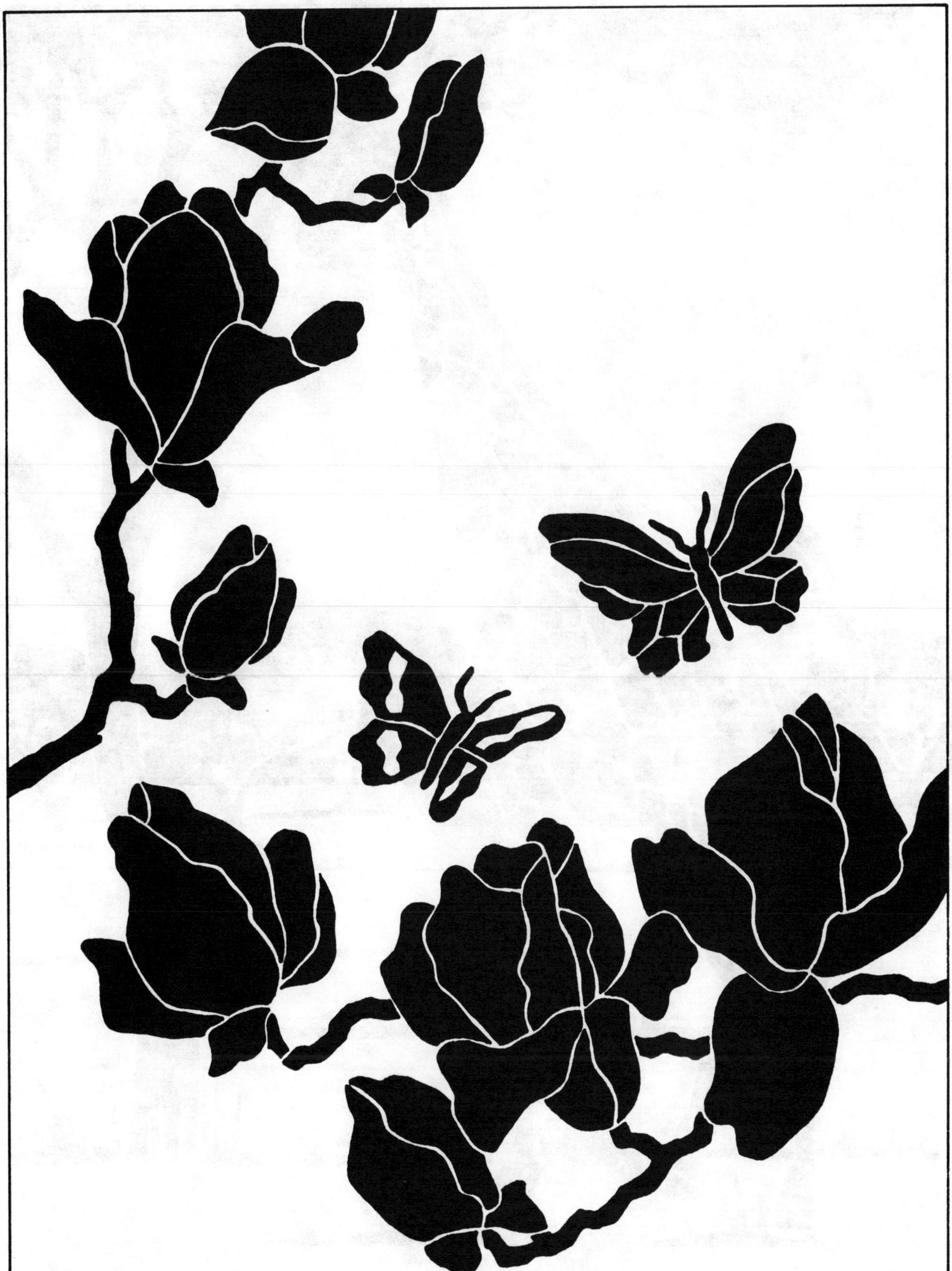

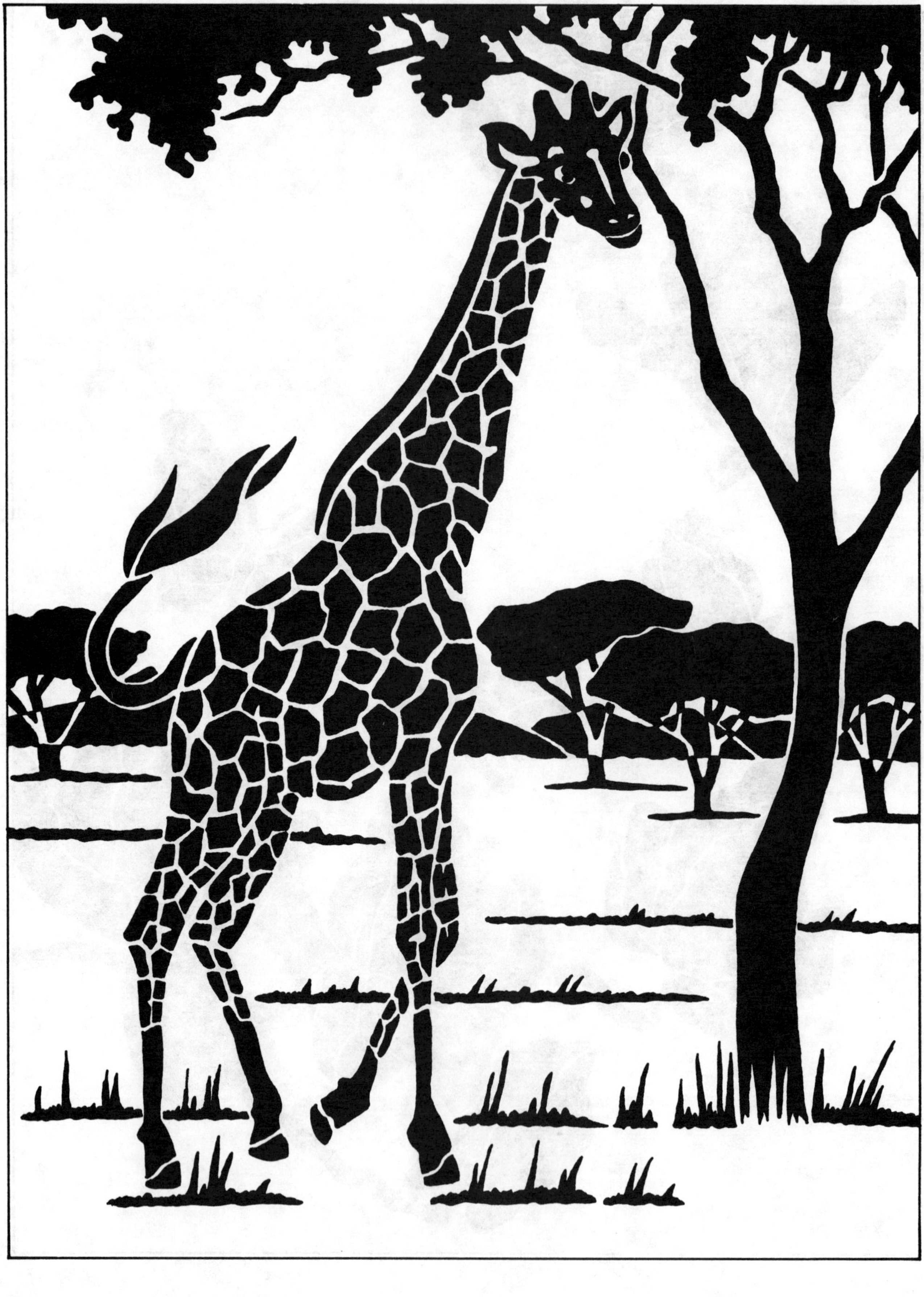

73

Background Scene

Create a Design Use the design segments on these and the next six pages to create your own designs. Enlarge the background scene to the size of your finished window. Then photocopy one or more of the birds provided, cut out and position on the enlarged scene. Use white-out or a white ink pen to outline wherever black areas meet. A fresh new design is ready to go.

75

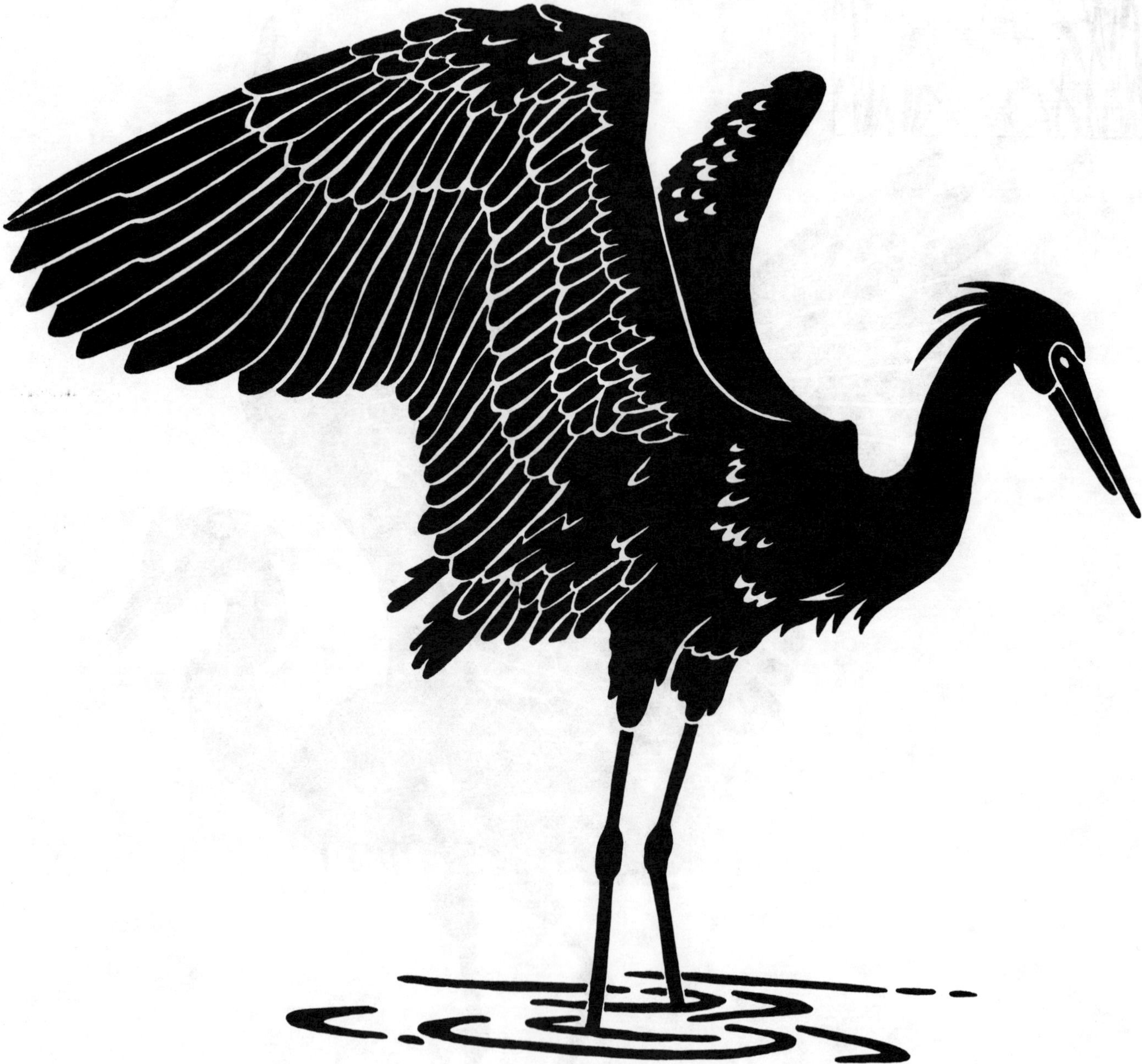

These birds are designed to fit into the basic scenes. They are also ideal for other etching jobs. Try them on bevels, mirrors, and other kinds of glass.

Background Scene

Size Relationships The larger the bird is made in proportion to the background scene, the more forward it will appear in the picture. Use this principle to create extra dimension and depth. This basic scene already has a start in that direction with the small birds flying above.

Positioning Placing the bird low in the scene will bring it forward and placing it higher will make it appear further away. Also experiment shifting it to the right and left for different kinds of balance.

Grouping Two or more birds can be overlapped in the same scene for a "group shot". (How ambitious you are at cutting resist may have some bearing on this decision.)

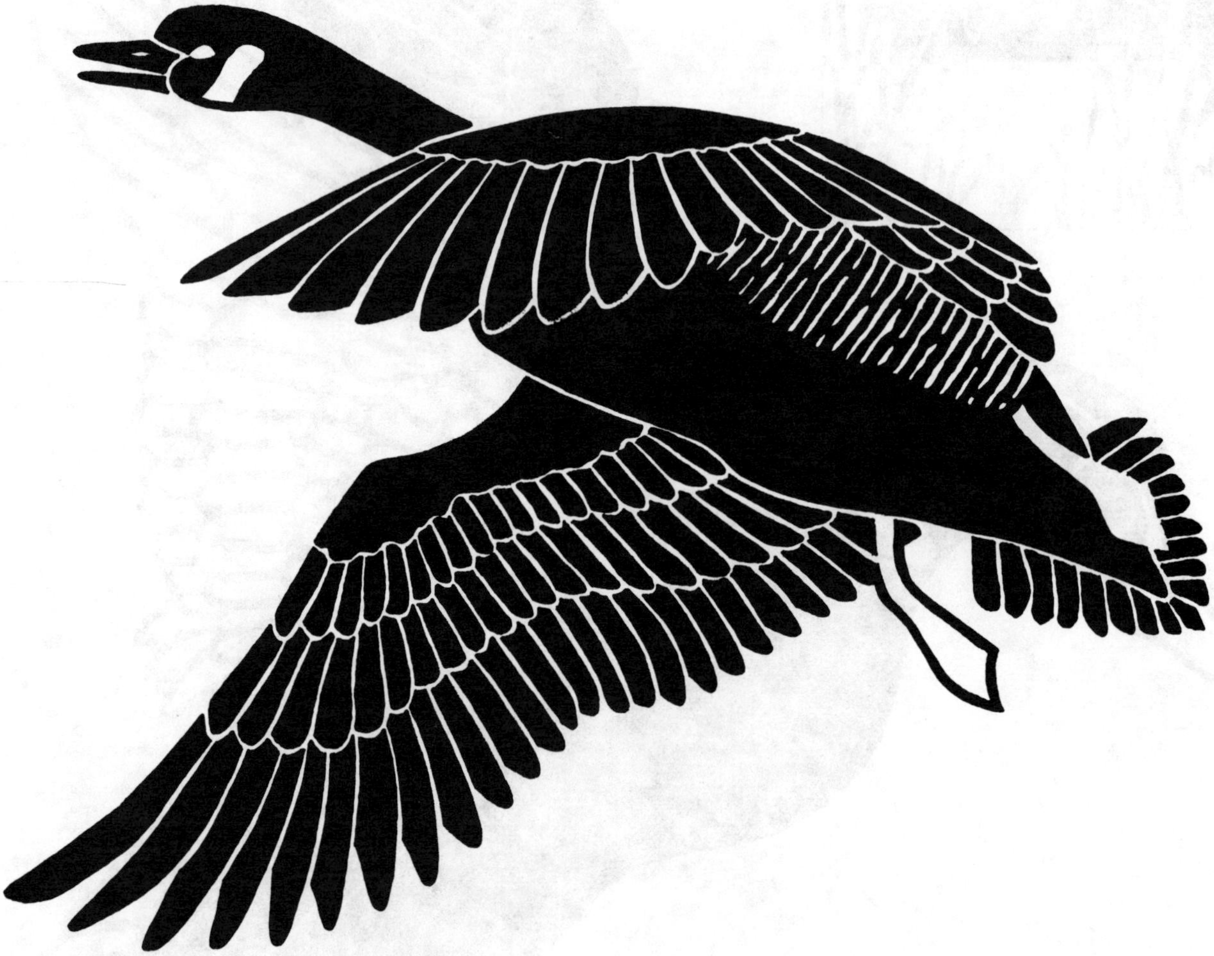

These birds are designed to fit into the basic scenes. They are also ideal for other etching jobs. Try them on bevels, mirrors, and other kinds of glass.

CKE-123 DRAGON
Full-size pattern information, page 96.

82

CKE-124 CHERRY BLOSSOMS
Full-size pattern information, page 96.

86

87

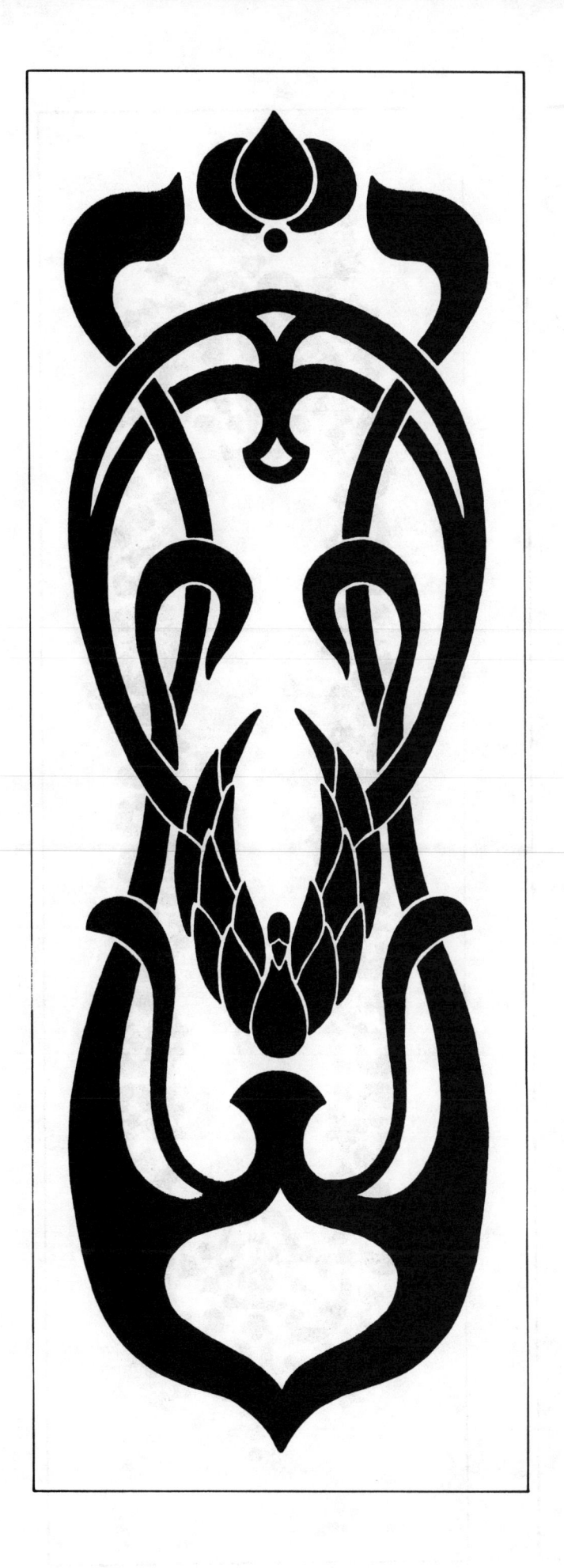

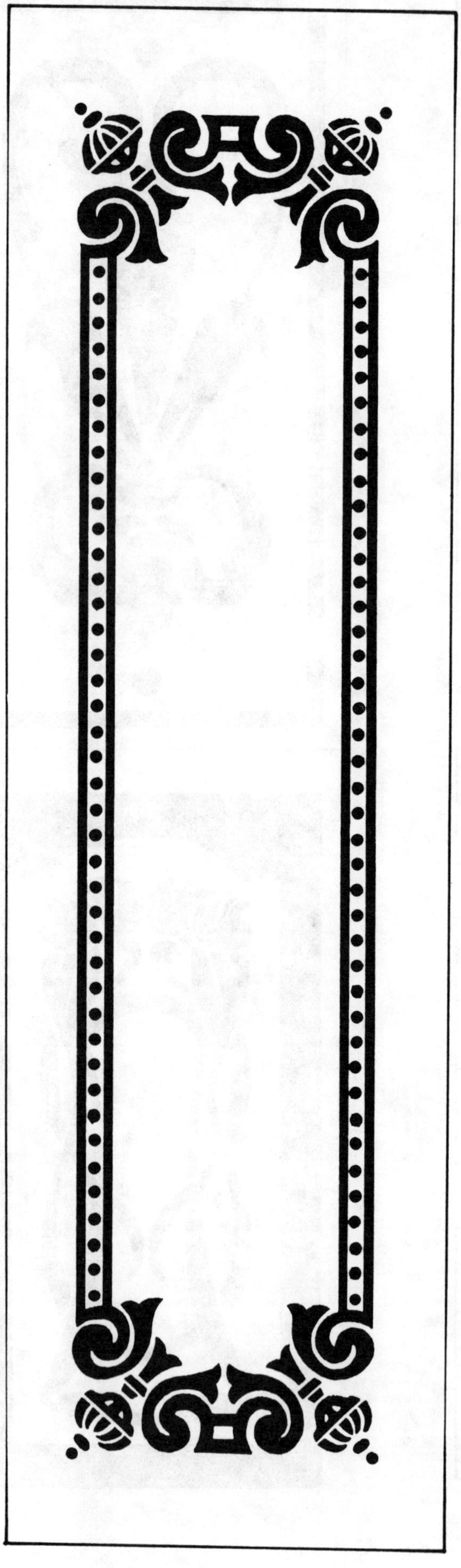

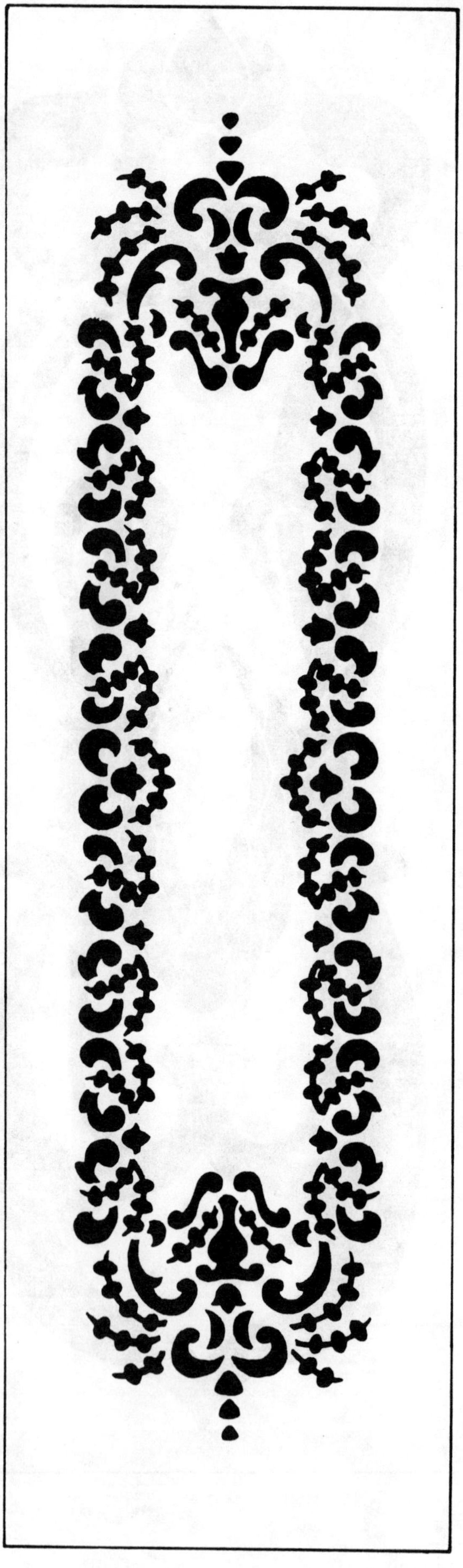

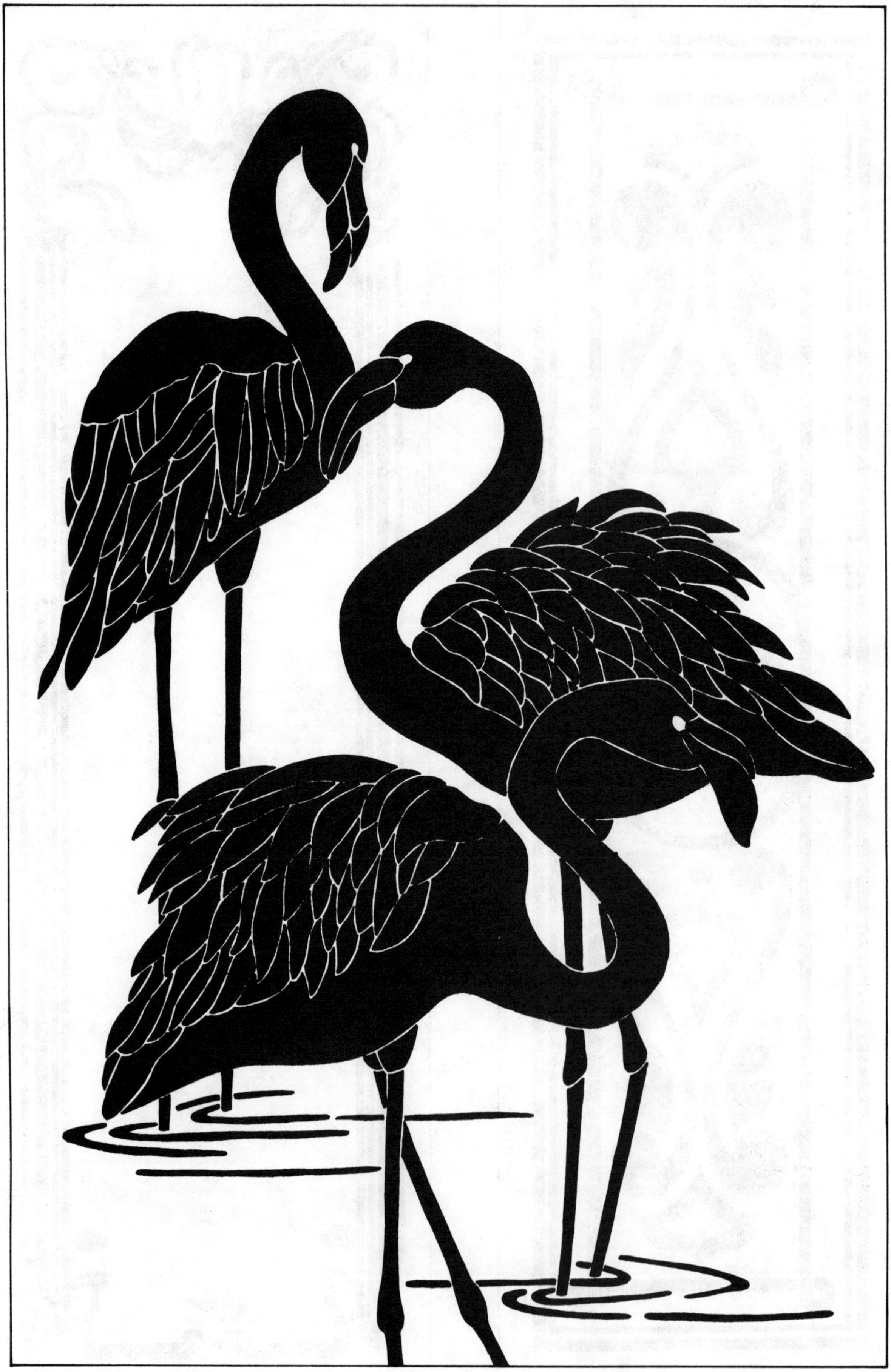

CKE-121 FISH SCENE    **CKE-122 SEAHORSE SCENE**

Full-size pattern information, page 96.

91

These three designs and the three designs on the next page are coordinated to be used individually, as pairs, or in groups of three.

Each one will stand by itself as an attractive sidelight or other good-sized window. The addition of one or more thin line borders with extra space beyond them would further enrich the design and be an ideal way to change the size of the full-size pattern.

Group any two designs that lie side-by-side on these pages to make double sidelights on each side of an entry door. Subject and line will flow from one window to the other and create a an elegant, unified entry.

The complete groups of three have been shown on the front cover and in the color section as free-standing screens. Each set can also be joined to make one large window by putting the patterns edge-to-edge and eliminating the dividing lines between them. (Some design redrawing will have to be done to compensate for the eliminated space between.

CKE-125 BAMBOO A

Full-size pattern information, page 96.

CKE-126 BAMBOO B

CKE-127 BAMBOO C

CKE-128 HERON A

CKE-129 HERON B

94

These designs and many others in the book take on a whole new look with a little thought and your own artistic input.

Very often just a section of a design will be the perfect subject to etch on a particular window or piece of glass. Following this idea a little further, a section of one design can be superimposed onto a section of another. Consider for example, placing one of the flamingos from the design on page 90 onto an upper foliage area from one of these designs. The combinations are quite endless and the final etching will be uniquely your own.

CKE-130 HERON C

Full-size pattern information, page 96.

95

Full-Size Patterns

Most of the designs in this book are already full-size or can be enlarged without too much difficulty. We have chosen to enlarge and separately package the ten designs below because they would be particularly good for sidelights and other large windows. One or more borders can be added to further enlarge the over-all design area.

Check with your local stained glass dealer for availability. If not available, send check or money order for $7.00 per pattern (includes postage and handling) to:

CKE PUBLICATIONS
2840-E Black Lake Blvd.
Olympia, WA 98502

PATTERN NUMBER:	PAGE NUMBER:	DESIGN TITLE:	PATTERN SIZE: (Inches)	(Centimeters)
CKE-121	91	Fish Scene	12" X 40"	30.5 X 101.5
CKE-122	91	Seahorse Scene	12" X 40"	30.5 X 101.5
CKE-123	82	Dragon	20" X 60"	50.8 X 152.4
CKE-124	83	Cherry Blossoms	20" X 60"	50.8 X 152.4
CKE-125	92	Bamboo A	22 1/2" X 58 1/2"	57.2 X 148.6
CKE-126	93	Bamboo B	22 1/2" X 58 1/2"	57.2 X 148.6
CKE-127	93	Bamboo C	22 1/2" X 58 1/2"	57.2 X 148.6
CKE-128	94	Heron A	22 1/2" X 58 1/2'	57.2 X 148.6
CKE-129	94	Heron B	22 1/2" X 58 1/2"	57.2 X 148.6
CKE-130	95	Heron C	22 1/2" X 58 1/2"	57.2 X 148.6

For information on Norman Dobbins etching video tapes, glass etching seminars and glass etching slide sets, please contact: National Sandblast Systems, Limited, 4421 Prospect N.E., Albuquerque, New Mexico 87110